THE BILLIONAIRE INSIDE YOUR HEAD

by Will Lord

SAMUEL FRENCH

FOR AMATEUR PRODUCTION ENQUIRIES

UNITED KINGDOM AND WORLD
EXCLUDING NORTH AMERICA
licensing@concordtheatricals.co.uk
020-7054-7298

Each title is subject to availability from Concord Theatricals,
depending upon country of performance.

This work is published by Samuel French, an imprint of Concord Theatricals Ltd.

The Professional Rights in this play are controlled by Sayle Screen Ltd, 11 Jubilee Place, London, SW3 3TD. Attn: Kelly Knatchbull.

USE OF COPYRIGHTED MUSIC

USE OF COPYRIGHTED THIRD-PARTY MATERIALS

IMPORTANT BILLING AND CREDIT REQUIREMENTS

NOTE

This edition reflects a rehearsal draft of the script and may differ from the final production.

THE BILLIONAIRE INSIDE YOUR HEAD was first performed at Hampstead Theatre Downstairs, London, on 19 September 2025. The cast and creative team were as follows:

RICHIE... Nathan Clarke
DARWIN .... Ashley Margolis
NICOLE/THE VOICE ....Allison McKenzie

Writer..Will Lord
Director .... Anna Ledwich
Designer.. Janet Bird
Lighting Designer .... James Whiteside
Sound Designer ....Max Pappenheim
Fight and Intimacy Directors ....Bethan Clark and Robin Helier
Stage Manager .... Em Cox

Hampstead Theatre champions the original, presenting world-class theatre on two ever-transforming stages.

Since its earliest incarnation in a simple hut over 60 years ago, Hampstead Theatre has always attracted outstanding talent, from Harold Pinter, Mike Leigh and Tom Stoppard to Nina Raine, Roy Williams and Beth Steel – innovators and original thinkers, every one.

As one of London's leading producing theatres, Hampstead Theatre showcases the very best of what's new; taking pride in the premiere of an astonishing debut, an inventive reimagining of an existing work, or an enthralled first-time audience member. It presents plays that are ingenious, surprising and accessible.

Hampstead Theatre's state-of-the-art home is in north west London, offering West End production values – but with tickets at a fraction of the cost. Hampstead believes in thought-provoking stories that are intelligently told, leaving audiences entertained and exhilarated.

hampsteadtheatre.com

CAST

NATHAN CLARKE | Richie

Nathan Trained at E15.

Theatre work includes *The Suicide* (National Theatre); *East is East* (Trafalgar Studios); *Pigeons* (Royal Court); *The Revenger's Tragedy* (Nottingham Playhouse); *Break the Floorboards* (Watford Palace); *Upstairs* (Finborough); *Small Fish Big Cheese* (Unicorn); *Thugz N Tearz* (Cockpit) and *La Ronde* (Tristan Bates).

Film work includes *Played and Betrayed, Sideshow, Thomas & Friends: Sodor's Legend of the Lost Treasure, We Still Know the Old Way, Harry Potter and the Half Blood Prince* and *Harry Potter and the Order of the Phoenix.*

Television work includes *Grace, Magpie Murders, Alex Rider, Tryant, The Duchess, Nasty Neighbours, The B@it, 4 O'Clock Club, The Interceptor, Casualty* and *Breakout 2050.*

Radio work includes *Dangerous Visions: Siege* (3 episodes).

ASHLEY MARGOLIS | Darwin

Theatre work includes *The Shark Is Broken* (UK & Ireland tour); *The Band's Visit* (Donmar) and *Bad Jews* (Arts Theatre).

Film work includes *A Christmas Number One.*

Short film work includes *Moon Rock, Two Minutes* and *The Doll's House.*

Television work includes *Brassic* (series 6), *Silent Witness* (series 27), *The VAR Room, Casualty, So Awkward, Holby City, The City and the City, Comedy Playhouse, Father Brown, Living the Dream, Some Girls* and *Hollyoaks.*

ALLISON MCKENZIE | Nicole

Theatre work includes *Red or Dead* (Royal Court); *In Shakespeare's Company* (RSC); *The Promise* and *The Butterfly Lion* (both Chichester Festival Theatre); *Wilderness* (Hampstead Theatre); *Seven Acts of Mercy, Two Noble Kinsmen* and *The Rover* (all RSC); *The Lion, The Witch and the Wardrobe* (Birmingham Rep); *Macbeth* (Trafalgar – Olivier Nomination); *Doctor in the House* (UK tour); *The Snow Queen* and *Hamlet* (both Lyceum Theatre); *Macbeth* (Nottingham Playhouse) *Witchcraft* (Finborough); *James and the Giant Peach* (Glasgow Citizens); *All My Sons* and *A Midsummer Night's Dream* (both Dundee Rep) and *Cabaret* (Dundee Rep – TMA nomination for Best Actress).

Film work includes *The Fall of Sir Douglas Weatherford, Swung, Airborne, New Town Killers, Club le Monde* and *16 Years of Alcohol.*

Television work includes *Outlander: Blood of my Blood, Our House, Crime, The Victim, Press, Shetland, Beowolf, Line of Duty, Bob Servant Independent* and *Rebus.*

CREATIVE

WILL LORD | Writer

Will is a screenwriter and playwright originally from Essex. *The Billionaire Inside Your Head* is his first stage play. He is a Mercury Playwright for 2025/26, and an alumnus of the London Library Emerging Writers Programme.

Will was a story producer on the recent ITV thriller *Code of Silence* starring Rose Ayling-Ellis, and upcoming BBC One drama *The Rapture*. As a script editor, his credits include *The Flatshare* and *The Girl Before*.

ANNA LEDWICH | Director

Previous work at Hampstead Theatre includes *Anthropology*, *Dry Powder* (Olivier Award nomination), *Labyrinth*, *Wilderness*, *Acceptance* (Olivier Award Best Comedy nomination), *Kiss Me* (also Trafalgar Studios), *The Argument*, *Four Minutes Twelve Seconds* (also Trafalgar Studios – Olivier Award for Outstanding Achievement in an Affiliate Theatre nomination), *Deluge, No One Will Tell Me How to Start a Revolution, The Empty Quarter* and *Donny's Brain*.

Other theatre work includes *Girls & Boys* (Nottingham Playhouse); *The Heartbreak Choir* and *Photograph 51* (both Ensemble Theatre, Sydney); *Coram Boy* (Chichester Festival Theatre); *Godzonia* (Q Theatre, Auckland); *Cookies* (Haymarket); *Roundelay* (Southwark Playhouse); *The Stick House* (Bristol Temple Meads Station); *How Does a Snake Shed its Skin* (BAC/Summerhall, Edinburgh); *Blue Remembered Hills* (Chichester Festival Theatre); *My House is Wallpapered with Lies* (Lyric); *Dream Story* (Gate); *Lulu* (Headlong, Gate); *A Christmas Carol* (Chichester Festival Theatre); *Lovely and Misfit* (Trafalgar Studios); *GBS* (Theatre503); *Roulette* (Finborough); *Poet No. 7* (Theatre503/Dublin Fringe Festival); *Pinocchio, The Butterfly Lion* and *Beauty and the Beast* (all Chichester Festival Theatre) and *Crossing Lines* (Chichester Festival Youth Theatre).

Work as Associate Director includes *All New People* (Duke of York's); *Private Lives* (Royal Alexandra Theatre, Toronto/Music Box Theatre, Broadway); *Six Characters in Search of an Author* (Headlong UK tour/ West End/Sydney International Festival/Perth International Festival) and *The Grapes of Wrath* (ETT, Birmingham Rep/West Yorkshire Playhouse).

JANET BIRD | Designer

Theatre work includes *Out of Season, 4 Minutes 12 Seconds, The Argument, Ken* and *Alphabetical Order* (all Hampstead Theatre); Girls and Boys (Nottingham Playhouse); *The Cabinet Minister* (Menier Chocolate Factory); *White Christmas, Guys and Dolls, The Wizard of Oz, Kiss Me Kate, Rock/Paper/Scissors, Talent* and *Hobson's Choice* (all Sheffield Crucible);

What's New Pussycat? (Birmingham Rep); *Rapunzel* and *Our Lady of Blundellsands* (both Liverpool Everyman); *Milky Peaks, Much Ado About Nothing* and *Cat on a Hot Tin Roof* (all Theatr Clwyd); *The Merry Wives of Windsor, The Comedy of Errors* and *Holding Fire* (all Shakespeare's Globe); *Hay Fever* (Guthrie, Minneapolis); *A Midsummer's Night's Dream* (Regent's Park); *The Madness of George III* (Apollo); *Enjoy* (Gielgud); *The Way Old Friends Do* (Criterion); *Uncle Vanya* (St James'); *The Rocky Horror Show* (Playhouse); *Abigail's Party* (UK tour); *History Boys* (UK tour); *Single Spies* (UK tour) and *Tell Me on a Sunday* (UK tour).

JAMES WHITESIDE | Lighting Designer

Recent work includes *Anthropology* and *The Dumb Waiter* (both Hampstead Theatre); *101 Dalmatians* (Apollo/UK tour); *Hey Christmas Tree, Pinocchio, The Midnight Gang, Miss Julie, Black Comedy, A Marvellous Year for Plums, The Ragged Trousered Philanthropists, Wallenstein* and *Funny Girl* (all Chichester Festival Theatre); *Stage Struck* and *The Spotlight Bar* (both Princess Cruises); *Bridgerton* and *Stranger Things* (both Secret Cinema); *The Last Tango, Dance Til Dawn, Midnight Tango, Never Forget* and *Footloose* (all UK tours/West End); *Hogarth's Progress* (Kingston Rose); *The Koala Who Could, Tango Moderno, Shirley Valentine* and *Love Me Tender* (all UK tours); *The Royale, Disgraced* and *Fear* (all Bush); *The Night Before Christmas* and *Little Sure Shot* (both Leeds Playhouse) and *Visitors, Far from the Madding Crowd, Plunder* and *Copenhagen* (all Watermill, Newbury).

Work for Tall Stories Theatre Company includes *The Gruffalo, The Gruffalo's Child, Room on the Broom* and *The Snail and the Whale*.

MAX PAPPENHEIM | Sound Designer

Recent theatre work includes *The Invention of Love* and *Labyrinth* (both Hampstead Theatre); *The Night of the Iguana* and *Cruise* (both West End); *The Children* (Broadway); *Noughts and Crosses* and *Twelfth Night* (both Regent's Park); *A Raisin in the Sun* (Headlong); *The Forsyte Saga* (Park); *The School for Scandal* and *Crooked Dances* (both RSC); *Coram Boy* and *Macbeth* (both Chichester Festival Theatre); *Shed: Exploded View* (Royal Exchange); *A Doll's House Part 2* and *The Way of the World* (both Donmar); *Village Idiot* and *One Night in Miami* (both Nottingham Playhouse); *Henry V* (Shakespeare's Globe/Headlong); *Hamlet* (Bristol Old Vic); *Ophelia Zimmer* (Schaubühne/Royal Court); *Not Your Superwoman* (Bush); *The Homecoming* and *My Cousin Rachel* (both Theatre Royal, Bath); *Creditors* and *Churchill in Moscow* (both Orange Tree).

Opera and Ballet work includes *The Limit* (Royal Ballet); *The Marriage of Figaro* (Salzburg Festival) and *Miranda* (Opéra Comique, Paris).

Associate Artist of Orange Tree Theatre, The Faction and Silent Opera. Off West End Award for Sound Design for *Old Bridge*.

BETHAN CLARK | Fight and Intimacy Director

Bethan is a Fight and Intimacy Director and certified senior teacher with the British Academy of Dramatic Combat.

Theatre work includes *Inside No. 9 Stage/Fright* (Wyndham's/UK tour); *Marie and Rosetta* (Kingston Rose/Chichester Festival Theatre/ETT); *The Merry Wives of Windsor, Romeo and Juliet* and *Princess Essex* (all Shakespeare's Globe); *A Streetcar Named Desire* (Sheffield Crucible); *Cowbois* (RSC/Royal Court); *The Hot Wing King, Dixon and Daughters* and *The Odyssey: The Underworld* (all National Theatre); *Dracula, Ghosts, Our Country's Good* and *Wedding Band: A Love Hate Story In Black and White* (all Lyric Hammersmith); *Lord of the Flies, Coram Boy* and *Cinderella* (all Chichester Festival Theatre); *The Ministry of Lesbian Affairs* (Kiln); *Brassed Off* (Theatre by the Lake); *Twelfth Night* (Shakespeare North Playhouse); *Wendy: A Peter Pan Story* (Theatre Royal, Bath); *Liberation* and *Romeo and Juliet* (both Manchester Royal Exchange); *The Swell* (Orange Tree) and *Othello* (Liverpool Everyman).

ROBIN HELLIER | Associate Fight and Intimacy Director

Theatre work includes *The 39 Steps, The Great Gatsby, Sunshine on Leith* and *Grease* (all Pitlochry Festival Theatre); *The Three Musketeers* (Shanghai Dramatic Arts Centre); *Dear Annie, I Hate You* (Pleasance/ Riverside Studios); *The Mosinee Project* (New Diorama); *Revenge: After the Levoyah* (Soho); *A Streetcar Named Desire* and *Group Portrait in a Summer Landscape* (both Lyceum Edinburgh/Pitlochry Festival Theatre); *The Trojan Women* and *Haemosporidian* (both Lyric Hammersmith); *Romeo & Juliet, The Merry Wives of Wishaw, Henry IV, Richard III, Hamlet, Henry V* and *As You Like It* (all Bard in the Botanics); *Little Women* (HOME Manchester); *The Witness* and *Macbeth* (both Avant Cymru Theatre Company); *My Brother's Keeper* (Theatre503); *Tosca* (Opera Bohemia) and *Macbeth, Faust: The Devil Went Down to Paisley* (both Paisley Opera).

Film work includes *We Few Survivors, Let's Get Out of The City, Kill Your Lover* and *Boudica*.

CHARACTERS

RICHIE – early/mid-twenties.

DARWIN – early/mid-twenties. Also portrays **STEPHANIE**, mid-twenties.

NICOLE – late forties/early fifties. Darwin's mother and Richie's boss.

THE VOICE – lives inside Richie's head. Played by the same actor as Nicole.

SETTING

The play mostly takes place in Richie & Darwin's basement office. The basement is a decaying, forgotten file room, the kind with a precariously dangling exposed lightbulb. Several huge filing cabinets adorn the space. Several health and safety laws are probably being broken by allowing them to work there.

Nicole's office and house should feel more modern and polished than the basement. Not a hair out of place.

The Voice's scenes take place in a liminal space, more imagined than defined.

TIME

Present day.

NOTES ON TEXT

' on its own line denotes a pause.

/ at the end of a line denotes two characters speaking over each other.

ACKNOWLEDGEMENTS

As I write this, we're one week into rehearsals with the Hampstead Theatre and an amazing company, and I am so grateful to all of them for trusting in this odd little play and helping make it into something real.

There are many others without whom this play wouldn't exist and all of them deserve a huge thank you. Firstly, countless very patient English teachers who never got as irritated as they could've with me, much appreciated.

To the friends and other writers who read numerous drafts and gave their very kind and vital feedback, thank you so much. Thank you also to my agent Kelly for being a wonderful collaborator and really believing in this.

This play was initially developed on the London Library Emerging Writers' programme, and a huge thank you goes to them for supporting new writing and letting me use their building and archive to work on basically whatever I wanted for a year. Which seems insane in hindsight.

Thank you to Jo, for telling me to write this play and insisting, despite my protesting to the contrary, that it was worth doing. I guess you might've had a point.

And last but definitely not least thank you to my parents. Not just for the whole creating me thing (very important) but also being lovely inspiring people and being all nice about the writing stuff. Thanks!!

Two books that really helped me as I was trying to write this and might be of interest to anyone who enjoyed this play are *The Man Who Couldn't Stop* by David Adam, and *The Will To Change* by bell hooks.

On average, it takes people seventeen years after the onset of their symptoms to receive an effective diagnosis and treatment for OCD. It took me eighteen to even mention it to anyone, or realise there was something unusual about the way my brain worked. So if something in this play resonated with you a little too much for comfort, it might be worth bringing it up to someone. I promise it will help.

Prologue

(THE VOICE bounds on with the energy of an 80s Zumba teacher. She is fully aware of us. Curious and excited, like a child who enjoys plucking the wings off flies.)

THE VOICE. Well I don't like how you're all staring at me.

That's a bit rude, isn't it. I'm not used to being looked at. Not sure I like it.

'

And you're really looking at *all* of me, aren't you? Up and down.

Shameless.

'

But get your shit together now, come on. I'm not used to being looked at, I'm used to being *listened to.*

Why don't you look at each other instead. Go on – I'm not kidding. Look at each other. Find someone across the room. Someone you don't know. Look them in the eyes. Now don't blink away, try and hold their gaze. "Ooh it's awkward!" I know, but just *try*, okay?

'

Well have you found someone now? Good. Keep looking at them. Now, answer nice and quick and out loud.

Would you fuck them?

Oh don't be childish about it, come on. Would you fuck them? It's a simple yes/no question.

Not right now – I mean feel free, but I think we'd all rather you stayed in your seats – but more hypothetically. At any point in your life, if the circumstances were to align, and it's on the table. Maybe it's on an actual table.

Would you fuck them?

,

I can sense some resistance to answering this question. But I've given you long enough to stare at them by now, haven't I? You've had a good look. Haven't you made up your mind?

What, now you've got to say it out loud you're all fucking shy? Come on, don't pretend you weren't thinking about it before I even asked. Staring at a stranger... little bit of you going "Nice". Or perhaps "Ugh". Don't pretend you weren't thinking about it looking at me. Looking at all of me. Looking me up and down and clearly not fucking *listening*.

Let's try it a different way. Look at your person. *Look* at them. Now imagine. It's five years in the future. If you're with someone now, sorry, they're dead. Or they started having a *lot* of 'yoga' sessions with Enrique and stopped coming home. I don't care. They're gone. You... are available.

You're in a bar. Or a library. Or maybe a vape shop? However people meet these days. Anyway. This person in front of you walks up and introduces themselves. They've been looking at you, you see. From across the bar, nursing their gin & tonic. Or their copy of *War & Peace*. Or their cherry mango Elf Bar.

And they wanted to say hi.

Now before you know it, you've been chatting for hours. You have so much in common. Or maybe you don't – maybe that excites you. But the bar's closing. The librarian's giving you a disapproving glare. The vape shop's being raided by police because it's a money laundering front because obviously it is because who goes to vape shops.

This person – the one you're supposed to be looking at – gives you a little touch on your arm. Maybe you've been out of the game for a while, but you know what that means.

So here we are. You've connected, you've found each other as two lost souls in the terrifying storm of life blah blah blah whatever. But at the end of the day you are fucking primates looking to continue your gene pool and you need to be *physically* attracted to someone. So look at the curves of their face. The curves of the rest of them. The clothes they're wearing. The kind of person you've assumed they are.

...so would you?

,

You understand I'm not asking you anything you haven't thought about before? It's all inside your head. I promise it is. Burning, folding, spinning. Would I fuck her, would I kill him, should I tell them I don't love them anymore. Will I ever find anyone or will I be alone forever? Will I ever be happy with myself? Am I destined for greatness or am I going to die alone in a ditch with nobody but hungry foxes to remember the taste of me?

Everything you want from your stupid little lives, everything you're afraid to want and afraid to say you want and afraid to even want to say...

It's all inside your head. And you've got to let me help you get it out. Because if you don't get it out I can promise you won't leave any mark on this world but vapid, empty breath.

So, for once in your lives, *listen*. When you lock eyes with someone, and I ask you if you'd fuck them...*give me an answer.*

,

Now I know some of you still feel 'a bit awkward'. "Oh no I feel like I'm judging this person unfairly that I've never met, it's rude to objectify people, isn't this harassment" Blah blah blah. "What if I don't want to say?"

What if you don't want to say? Then I'll have to decide for you.

> *(Now her demeanour changes. Her temperature drops. She's ready to pluck off some wings.)*

Maybe I'll make you have sex with them. Maybe you'll have to. Maybe you'll find yourself under them, disgusted, knowing that all you had to do to avoid this was to fucking say what you want.

,

Or maybe...maybe I'll make them your soulmate. Your one true love. God, it's magical isn't it? They're everything you ever dreamed of. You're so deliriously happy – they've given your life meaning again. You won't die alone. You're not a pointless, fleeting speck of dust. You're in *looooooove.*

But when you lie them down on your bed, and you lean in for that perfect kiss on those perfect lips, thinking of everything you could do to each other...you stop. They're confused – "is everything alright honey?" But you don't move. And you don't say anything. Because you know, deep down. You remember this moment, when you didn't say, and you *know.*

That I won't ever let you fuck them. *Ever.*

,

Tell me, how's that sound?

> *(Blackout.)*

1.

(The basement is a decaying, forgotten file room, the kind with a precariously dangling exposed lightbulb.)

(Several huge filing cabinets sit behind their desks, looming. They will often be searched for a particular file, but the right one will never, ever be found.)

*(**RICHIE** and **DARWIN** are sitting at their desks. **RICHIE** is, ostensibly, working through a file. **DARWIN** smokes a large joint. He does not offer it to **RICHIE**. They are mid-argument.)*

RICHIE. – I'm just saying there's a work ethic there, right. No matter what position he's in now he's worked his arse off to get there. His family wasn't rich –

DARWIN. Piss off his family wasn't rich. They owned an *emerald mine.*

Have you seen the the Paulsen file?

*(**RICHIE** looks around but shakes his head. **DARWIN** searches his desk.)*

RICHIE. I know it sounds bad but an emerald mine in South Africa then didn't cost that much. You think emerald mine you think supervillain private island but actually it was an ordinary middle-class business investment, like a second home.

DARWIN. What, "darling shall we pop down to the mine this weekend?"

(Back looking for the file.) It was right here...

> **(RICHIE** *chuckles.* **DARWIN** *looks at the papers in front of him.)*

Actually do you want to take this one? Paulsen. It sounds boring as shite. Go on. I bet you can find it too.

RICHIE. What? No, I've just started mine. Anyway you know we can't swap the ones we're allocated. It looks bad.

DARWIN. Who cares?

RICHIE. Easy for you to say mate.

DARWIN. What's that mean?

> *(Beat.* **RICHIE** *shakes his head, grinning.)*

Oh come on you love this complex maths shit, it'll do my head in. I want a nice simple trail and an address.

RICHIE. It wouldn't do your head in if you weren't stoned every morning.

DARWIN. I'm not stoned, I'm invulnerable. It's my version of coffee. You're allowed a drug in the morning why can't I?

Come on pleaaaaase swap.

RICHIE. Nooooope.

> **(DARWIN** *sighs and begins to search for the Paulsen file in the filing cabinets.)*

DARWIN. Well, most people don't have second homes. However much it cost it's an advantage –

RICHIE. I know most people don't but lots of people do and they don't all go on to become the richest man in the world do they?! I'm just saying *clearly* there's something special about him –

DARWIN. And I'm just saying stop trying to suck his dick/

RICHIE. Just because his family wasn't living in a slum doesn't mean he doesn't deserve everything he's earned/

DARWIN. Stop trying to suck his dick. Stop trying to suck his weird pasty apartheid-Clyde jewel-mining dick and where the fuck is this file?!

RICHIE. Just because they were white doesn't mean they benefitted that much from –

(*Off* **DARWIN**'s *look.*) Okay fine but –

DARWIN. Just because he makes a few cars that literally *catch fire* doesn't mean he's the pinnacle of human civilisation, also isn't he basically a Nazi now?

RICHIE. I know he has gone a bit off the deep end, but –

DARWIN. A bit?! You sound like a fucking incel, stop trying to suck –

RICHIE. You know that's actually quite homophobic of you, just because I *admire* another man's *drive* doesn't mean I want to suck his dick.

(*Beat. They both grin.*)

Now if you'll excuse me, I need to find the last known address of Mister Tommy Fox because he now owes your Mum...

(*He checks the file and whistles softly.*)

A cool ten grand. Damn.

(*Beat.*)

DARWIN. Ay don't say it like that though.

RICHIE. Like what?

DARWIN. Like he "owes my Mum" like she's fucking Wonga.com. It wasn't her who lent him money. She's just...

RICHIE. How would you put it?

DARWIN. I don't know, like we're stuck in an asbestos looking basement chasing down people who probably don't exist anymore. I don't even understand how you can buy debt.

RICHIE. We went over this, it's sold as pennies to the pound that's why all those suits invested in it because the profit margins are unbelievable –

DARWIN. BUT IT'S SO BOOORING.

RICHIE. Ey isn't it fun to have a baller for a Mum now though?

> (**DARWIN** *looks a bit uncomfortable.* **RICHIE** *goes back to his file.* **DARWIN** *continues searching, fruitlessly. Eventually he gives up, slams the cabinet closed.)*

> (*He's bored now. He ambles round* **RICHIE**. *Gives him a poke.)*

Nah man I actually gotta finish this. Unlike you I care about my performance targets.

DARWIN. Come oooon it's only eleven a.m.!

> (**DARWIN** *pokes him again. No reaction.)*

RICHIE. For real man, let me finish.

> (*Beat.* **DARWIN** *reaches out and 'grabs'* **RICHIE**'*s nose, poking his thumb through his fingers as the 'nose'.)*

Did you just got-your-nose me?

DARWIN. I did.

RICHIE. Are you twelve?

DARWIN. Apparently.

> (**DARWIN** *bursts out laughing.* **RICHIE** *laughs too, but it seems a little forced.*)

Now what are we thinking for lunch? I read there's a new meal deal selection at Tesco if you wanna give it the official inspection.

> (**RICHIE** *says nothing. Beat.* **DARWIN** *stops – sensing something's slightly off.*)

What?

RICHIE. Nah, nothing.

,

Just erm...

Can I...can I have my nose back?

> (*Beat.*)

DARWIN. What?

RICHIE. Nose. Can I have my nose back?

DARWIN. Your nose.

RICHIE. Yeah, you did the thing... you took it off –

> (*Beat.*)

DARWIN. It's on your face mate.

RICHIE. No I know it is, I know it's there, I just...I just need you to put it back, I know it's weird, I know I'm being...

DARWIN. Is this one of your...one of your things?

RICHIE. I guess. I dunno, maybe/

DARWIN. Cos I remember this, I remember this from when we were at school you used to do this/

(**DARWIN** *starts to crack up.*)

DARWIN. I promise I didn't actually rip it off your face –

RICHIE. No I know man, I know it's not real/

DARWIN. There'd be blood everywhere, it wouldn't be pretty/

RICHIE. I know it's really still there, I just need you to put it back. Okay? Please.

(**DARWIN** *snorts. Beat. Then he shrugs and mimes putting* **RICHIE***'s nose back.*)

No, you dropped it, remember?

DARWIN. What now?

RICHIE. It's not in your hand. When you stopped holding it, you dropped it.

(**DARWIN** *is nonplussed. After a beat* **RICHIE** *points to the floor.*)

It's over there right?

(*Beat.* **DARWIN** *looks at the empty floor.*)

DARWIN. Right. Guess it is.

(**DARWIN** *bends down and picks up the 'nose', putting his thumb between his fingers. He brushes dirt off it, straight-faced, then slowly slots it back onto* **RICHIE***'s face.*)

RICHIE. Thanks.

(*A long beat. Then* **DARWIN** *bursts out laughing hysterically.*)

DARWIN. Mate you have got to stop this shit now. You're like, in your twenties.

RICHIE. You're the one who got-your-nosed me!!

DARWIN. My childhood regression is charming and endearing! Yours is just being fucking weird all the time.

*(Beat. Laughing too, **RICHIE** leaps up, eager to change the subject.)*

RICHIE. Right, you're bored? You know what we need to do.

DARWIN. What?

*(**RICHIE** starts enthusiastically doing star-jumps.)*

DARWIN. You know what I just said about being a weirdo.

RICHIE. Trust. You just need to get your endorphins flowing, your energy up, then you'll be motivated to grind out the rest of the day. It's a *performance catalyst*.

DARWIN. Why do I get the feeling this is what your best pal Elon does?

RICHIE. It doesn't have to be long. Jack Dorsey just does a seven-minute workout in the morning. Gets the brain pumping.

DARWIN. Who is Jack Horsey?

*(**RICHIE** stops.)*

RICHIE. Founder of Twitter. Sorry –

(He crosses his arms like this guy: 🧟)

'X'. Look, it's work. It doesn't matter if you don't love reading files, you gotta smash it anyway.

*(Off **DARWIN**'s look.)*

Okay fine, let's make it more...

*(He grabs his phone and puts on music –
"I Got Ants In My Pants (And I Need To Dance)"
by James Brown.* He moves in a surprisingly
assured two-step. Hips swinging. No finger-
guns-straight-man-at-the-club dancing here.)*

RICHIE. Come on, do you trust me? I know you do. You
know the Godfather wants you to dance.

*(Under pressure, **DARWIN** sighs and starts
to dance too, a little more stilted. Maybe they
fall into a two-step together, side to side.)*

Yeaaaah that's right. Get every part of your body moving.

James Brown. Hardest working man in show business.
You know he drilled his band so tight if they made a
mistake during a show, he'd hear it and hold up his
fingers, and that's how much he'd dock their salary.
Missed a dance move? Twenty-five bucks. Messed up
the end of a song? Fifty dollars.

DARWIN. That's pretty brutal.

RICHIE. Maybe. But you end up with a groove this good...
might be worth it.

(He spins round.)

Can you feel it yet?

*(**DARWIN** laughs and smiles.)*

DARWIN. You know what, a little.

RICHIE. You feel ready to chase down some DEBTS?

DARWIN. I guess.

---

* A licence to produce *The Billionaire Inside Your Head* does not include
a performance licence for any third-party or copyrighted music or
copyrighted recordings. For further information, please see the Music
and Third-Party Materials Use Note on page iii.

RICHIE. Nah come on say it with me. Yell it. They can't hear upstairs. ARE YOU READY?!

DARWIN. Yeah!

RICHIE. LOUDER!

DARWIN. YEAH!

RICHIE. *(Beating his chest in time.)* FUCK YEAH?

DARWIN. FUCK YEAH!

> *(They both beat their chest, hollering.* **RICHIE** *pulls a surprised* **DARWIN** *in for a hug, slapping his back. Holding him there.* **DARWIN** *struggles a bit. Maybe he protests to let him go. Maybe he just squirms. After a little, he wriggles free and stands apart.)*

DARWIN. Alright, alright.

RICHIE. Alright. Now you're working like a fucking winner.

> *(They both settle down to their desks. After a few seconds, they look at each other and burst out laughing.)*
>
> *(Blackout.)*

2.

*(A clean office, many floors higher than the decaying basement. **RICHIE** seated. **NICOLE** comes in, talking quietly on her AirPods. She may look identical to **THE VOICE**, but she's from another planet. Business-focused. Gives nothing away. Every smile is stillborn behind the eyes.)*

*(She gives a 'one moment' gesture to **RICHIE**. He gives an enthusiastic thumbs up. **NICOLE** slaps a file down on the desk and turns her back. **RICHIE** notices – presumably his file. He strains to read it but it's too far. He slaps his thighs a little nervously.)*

*(Then he looks at **NICOLE**. Looks her up and down.)*

RICHIE. *(Murmuring.)* Yeah.

,

Yeah, I'd fuck her.

*(**NICOLE** turns, a 'did you say something' expression on her face. **RICHIE** shakes his head – 'nothing'. **NICOLE** finishes the call and hangs up.)*

NICOLE. Sorry about that, Rich. Welcome, welcome.

*(**RICHIE** jumps up and shakes her hand enthusiastically.)*

RICHIE. Yeah, thanks for having me, up in the penthouse...

(They both sit.)

You know it's actually been ages. You should come visit our basement kingdom sometime.

NICOLE. Oh really? It's a long trip down. What is it, forty floors?

RICHIE. We've decorated though, it's quite the palace now yeah

NICOLE. Tell me you haven't made it some kind of man cave.

RICHIE. *(Laughing.)* Nah nah just a proper productive work environment. Promise!

NICOLE. Good because I remember Darwin's room and I cannot be near that smell ever again. Teenage boys, I swear. And you had that *horrific* deodorant. Didn't your Mum ever complain?

> (**RICHIE** *laughs and shakes his head.*)

Well her nose must've been blocked. Shall we get on with it?

RICHIE. Yeah I just wanted to say how gr–

NICOLE. *(Cutting him off.)* Wait wait, let me do my spiel.

> (**RICHIE** *nods, grinning.*)

We do these every six months. Nothing to worry about, just a little chat to make sure everyone's achieving their personal goals, hitting performance targets. Checking everyone's still a fit for the team.

So.

> (*She opens the file – with a grin, like 'look at how ridiculous this is'.*)

We've been really impressed with your progress, Rich. Genuinely.

RICHIE. Thanks Nicole. Thank you.

NICOLE. Really impressed. Client tracing isn't easy, but it seems to be to you. It's a bit like being thrown in at the deep end –

RICHIE. But I like being thrown in at the deep end!

NICOLE. Clearly. You've made massive strides forward and honestly, that's about it. No feedback. Keep doing you.

    (**RICHIE** *smiles, nods.*)

The other thing is that I wanted to give you a cheeky heads up. There's going to be some...restructuring coming up, and as part of that we're recruiting for a new Junior Associate.

Now we'd really like to train someone up internally, if you get my meaning. It's a big step up, but a big opportunity. So we're going to invite all six of you Researchers to apply later this week.

But I wanted to let you know now. Our...little secret, if you like.

RICHIE. Wow. Yeah, fuck yeah, sorry... I'm in.

Big raise?

NICOLE. Careful!

    (*She leans forward conspiratorially.*)

But yes it is.

RICHIE. Nicole thank you, honestly I'm so grateful for this.

NICOLE. Course. You forget Rich, I've known you since you were in nappies. I know what your potential is. And this is a role we really need to go to the *right* person.

RICHIE. Totally. And like, you know I'm a hard worker. Really. I'll put in the hours, late nights, early mornings. A lot of people in my generation just wanna phone it in –

NICOLE. You talking about my son?

RICHIE. (*Laughing.*) No! No, not D but... you know people don't have the graft anymore. They don't have what you had.

NICOLE. Oh, and what did I have?

RICHIE. You knew where you wanted to be and you understood how hard you had to fucking grind until you got there. Right?

NICOLE. True.

RICHIE. I wanna run my own, my own company yeah, but I know it's gonna be sleepless nights and rejections and nothing nothing nothing until it finally pays off. And I'm ready, I'm committed to that.

And really Nicole I don't know if I ever said this to you but you're such an, an inspiration to me –

NICOLE. That's very sweet of you, Rich.

RICHIE. Nah but seriously, like as a businesswoman, everything you overcame to get here, all that adversity and you didn't even blink.

NICOLE. Adversity?

RICHIE. Well yeah I just, I imagine it wasn't easy, being a a woman, at that time, must've been... I can't imagine how difficult it was.

NICOLE. You can imagine or you can't imagine?

(*Beat.*)

RICHIE. I just mean like, I dunno. It must've been hard to... you had Darwin so young and you were still just starting out, maybe it was...hard to be taken seriously

NICOLE. You think I'm hard to take seriously?

RICHIE. No! No, the opposite, I was fucking terrified of you as a kid –

NICOLE. So I'm terrifying.

RICHIE. Fuck, sorry, no.

I just mean it's inspiring like back then you didn't have much and you were a woman and...and I imagine there's a lot of shit that comes with that, but you didn't let it get you down. I mean you never had help or a nanny or anything and it weren't like Darwin's dad was...

Like I remember when it first took off you started picking Darwin up wearing those grey business suits with the blazers cos you'd just come from meetings and...

> (**NICOLE** *raises her eyebrows and* **RICHIE** *tails off, unsure what point he was trying to make.*)

Sorry.

> (**NICOLE** *smiles. She starts packing up the file and stands.*)

NICOLE. Thanks for coming up.

RICHIE. Nicole can I ask actually, who was *your* inspiration? Like when you got started, who did you look up to?

> (*Beat.*)

NICOLE. I'm late for a meeting, Rich.

> (*Blackout.*)

3.

*(The basement. **RICHIE** sipping his morning coffee. **DARWIN** finishing his morning joint.)*

DARWIN. You're serious?

RICHIE. Swear down, she was all "I want a man who provides for me".

DARWIN. On a first date?

RICHIE. Bro, within ten minutes.

DARWIN. What did you say?

RICHIE. I leaned right in, I said "if you play your cards right tonight, I'll *provide* you anything you want." Then I signal the waitress real casual like –

(He holds up his hand nonchalantly.)

And she's right there and I'm like "starting with two glasses of red" you know red's got that bougie vibe right and I even pick one out from the menu. Said I'd had it before. Said I liked the tannins.

DARWIN. Alright, alright I see you!

What are tannins?

RICHIE. No idea.

(They laugh.)

DARWIN. Smooth. And she's looking good?

RICHIE. She's beautiful. But I'm not there for that right I'm there for long term. Like, is there a future here?

DARWIN. Oh sure you are, you're all, "I just wanna get to know your personality" –

RICHIE. You wanna hear this story or not?

RICHIE. So she's smiling but she doubles down like... kinda like...

> (**DARWIN** *steps into character as Richie's date,* **STEPHANIE**. *She is stylish, composed, exact.*)

DARWIN. *(As* **STEPHANIE**.*)* You know I'm serious though? He gotta be classy, good taste for fine things, willing to travel.

RICHIE. Just like that!

DARWIN. So what'd you say?

RICHIE. Told her that's not a problem.

DARWIN. *(As* **STEPHANIE**.*)* Oh really? Why's that?

RICHIE. Cos I'm gonna be a billionaire.

You're looking at the next Mark Zuckerberg.

> (**DARWIN** *switches back to himself.*)

DARWIN. No you did not say that, cringe cringe criiiiiiinge.

RICHIE. That's not cringe... is it? It's not. Is it?

DARWIN. Yes! It's so fucking tech bro.

RICHIE. I thought the confidence was kinda sexy.

DARWIN. Do you think of Mark Zuckerberg as sexy?

> *(Beat.)*

RICHIE. That's not the...

,

Shit.

> (**DARWIN** *bursts out laughing.*)

Shut uppp dickhead, I ain't taking dating advice from you.

(A comfortable beat.)

DARWIN. Why d'you keep telling people that anyway? That you're going to be a billionaire.

RICHIE. Because it's true.

(Beat.)

DARWIN. Okay.

RICHIE. I'm serious. It's the dream.

DARWIN. Yeah, when we were kids.

RICHIE. *(Teasing.)* Just cos you got that family money now, some of us have still gotta work for a living, eh.

DARWIN. My 'family money' literally pays your salary.

RICHIE. *(Prostrating himself.)* And I am most grateful for the charity of the superrich.

DARWIN. Shut up man. So go on, you're telling her you wanna be some super-nerd with a terrible haircut. Did it go down well?

RICHIE. Well she laughs right, but she hits back like –

DARWIN. *(As* **STEPHANIE**.*)* Do you use that line a lot?

RICHIE. First time. I swear. Is it working?

Or am I too good-looking for that comparison?

DARWIN. *(As* **STEPHANIE**, *laughs, looking him up and down.)* Maybe.

(Beat. Eye contact. **RICHIE** *moves it along –)*

RICHIE. So what's all this "I wanna be provided for"? Strong opener on a date, bit 1950s. Doesn't it scare a lot of guys off?

DARWIN. *(As* **STEPHANIE**.*)* Maybe that's the idea. You scared?

RICHIE. Me? Nah.

Well, a little. So is it like, a test?

DARWIN. *(As* **STEPHANIE**.*)* Can I be honest?

(**RICHIE** *nods.*)

I just don't wanna work.

RICHIE. You don't wanna work.

DARWIN. *(As* **STEPHANIE**.*)* Why should I?

(**RICHIE** *laughs.*)

I'm serious.

RICHIE. That's...

DARWIN. *(As* **STEPHANIE**.*)* You think I'm lazy now.

RICHIE. No... I think it's...

It's the whole deal, though. We work, we get money, we can do the things we wanna do. Enjoy life. You can't just ignore that.

DARWIN. *(As* **STEPHANIE**.*)* Why not? Am I hurting anyone?

RICHIE. Don't you have like, dreams? Achievements, some bucket list?

DARWIN. *(As* **STEPHANIE**.*)* I do. But it's not a career. It's... food. Friendships. Travel. Art. Things that need space and time outside a nine-to-five.

RICHIE. Well you gotta have money for them, are you planning to starve –

DARWIN. *(As* **STEPHANIE**.*)* That's where my rich billionaire comes in. Providing for me.

RICHIE. You got it all planned out, haven't you?

DARWIN. *(As* **STEPHANIE**.*)* Just like you have.

,

Look I'm no freeloader. Just because I won't earn money doesn't mean I won't provide for my partner too. I will. I'm the opposite of lazy. I just, have a different focus.

RICHIE. I guess I could get behind that.

DARWIN. *(As* **STEPHANIE.***)* Your turn then. Why do you wanna become a billionaire?

RICHIE. So I can treat beautiful women like you to what you deserve.

DARWIN. *(As* **STEPHANIE.***)* Haaaah okay, you're verging on corny now.

RICHIE. Pulling it back, I'm pulling it back.

,

Nah, I always wanted it. I mean, doesn't everyone?

I know I know, you don't wanna work, I get it. But think about it. You can have your food, your travelling, art or whatever. All of it. You'd have the best possible version of anything you wanted. And talk about friendships? How about every party you walk into, everyone just turns and smiles whether they like you or not! Cos who's gonna risk pissing you off, when you paid for the fucking thing?!

And every day you'd wake up like, with everything just...sorted. Just like the day before. You'd never have to worry about anything.

DARWIN. *(As* **STEPHANIE.***)* Do you worry about things?

(A beat that goes on for slightly too long.)

RICHIE. Doesn't matter now I'm a billionaire does it. I can just...click my fingers and summon another yacht to fix the problem.

Come on, wouldn't it be kinda fun?

DARWIN. *(As* **STEPHANIE,** *finishing the wine.)* I guess a yacht might be a little fun.

DARWIN. *(As* STEPHANIE.*)* But it's ethically impossible, right, to be a billionaire. You're always gonna be exploiting someone down the line.

RICHIE. *(Teasing.)* Oh you're one of thooose!

Maybe once. But this is the future we're talking about. There won't be a factory, there aren't any underpaid workers. I'm coming up with ideas, not even physical products, and letting investors decide how much to value them at. Just me...and the markets.

> (**DARWIN** *sits back, considering. Is [s]he impressed?)*

DARWIN. *(As* STEPHANIE.*)* You're a generous guy, aren't you Richie?

> *(He holds out his wine glass and* RICHIE *fills it up from the bottle.)*

Yeah. I can tell you like giving.

RICHIE. I guess I do.

DARWIN. *(As* STEPHANIE, *leaning in.)* Does it make you feel like the big man?

RICHIE. What?

DARWIN. *(As* STEPHANIE.*)* Do you feel good? Paying for my meal. Picking out my wine. Does it make you feel in charge?

RICHIE. Not...not in charge. I... no, it's just...

DARWIN. *(As* STEPHANIE.*)* It's okay. I like it. You're in control.

> (**RICHIE** *is a bit on edge but looks around the room and seems to settle.)*

RICHIE. Yeah. Yeah. I am.

DARWIN. *(As* STEPHANIE.*)* Good.

I wonder what else you could give me.

(He takes a coy sip of wine and looks away. His hand moves between them, upturned.)

Being so...generous.

*(Beat. **RICHIE** stretches out his hand to meet **DARWIN**'s. Their fingers graze. It's electric.)*

*(Then **DARWIN** snaps back to himself. They withdraw their hands suddenly. **DARWIN** jumps up.)*

Oh SHIT she did not say that?!

RICHIE. Yeah man, it's fucking wild. Well forward.

DARWIN. Soooo... Was it your place or hers? I know you don't wash your sheets so –

RICHIE. Nah, it weren't like that. I really like her, wanna take it slow.

DARWIN. Never in a million years have you liked a woman and taken it slow. You're normally considering marriage by now. What happened?

(Beat.)

RICHIE. Nothing, it just... I dunno the vibe was off at the end.

DARWIN. Oh what did you do, you twat?

RICHIE. Nothing! I didn't do anything!

DARWIN. Bullshit you didn't. Did you forget her name? Or get a boner. Or, oh did you try and talk about how much of a feminist you are again because fuck I remember how horrible that was –

RICHIE. No!

*(Beat. **DARWIN** stares at **RICHIE** until he gives in.)*

Fine. You remember the waitress?

DARWIN. Yeah.

RICHIE. Well I noticed her, she was, she was looking good herself, beautiful. And I didn't make eyes or do anything. Obviously.

DARWIN. Obviously. But...

RICHIE. So Stephanie, that's the girl, she gets all flirty right and then she gets a text and she's checking it.

And I'm nervous. I mean I'm...course I am. She's forward, she's sexy, she's smart, I'm like wow. And I think I'm gonna get to be generous to her tonight, you know?

DARWIN. Gross but continue.

RICHIE. So I'm looking around, heart beating fast like, and I see the waitress and I... well I swear I was talking under my breath so she couldn't hear but I said "Yeah".

DARWIN. You said "yeah"?

(**RICHIE** *takes a deep breath.*)

RICHIE. I said "Yeah".

,

"Yeah, I'd fuck her".

DARWIN. About the *waitress*?

RICHIE. Yeah.

DARWIN. Dude!

RICHIE. I know but I wasn't... I didn't mean it... I was just... it made me less nervous.

But Stephanie she hears and is like "what did you just say" and I tried to play it off but she definitely heard and she didn't *say* anything but...

I dunno she called it a night pretty soon after that. Felt done to be honest.

DARWIN. What did the waitress say?

RICHIE. I don't think she heard.

　　(Beat.)

DARWIN. Mate can you explain to me what the fuck was going through your head because/

RICHIE. Can we just get back to work now? I need to find the other Tommy Fox files/

　　*(**DARWIN** stares as **RICHIE** gets up and begins to search through the filing cabinets.)*

DARWIN. Richie –

RICHIE. I don't wanna go into it, okay?

　　*(**RICHIE** searches the cabinets for some time. **DARWIN** waits, not finished. Unfortunately, **RICHIE**'s file never shows up. He gets frustrated. Maybe he hits the cabinet. Eventually, file unfound, he sits down, defeated.)*

I just get a bit nervous on dates like, when it seems something's going really well, when you really click with someone you know?

Like when things are going well I'm on edge, like what if this is it what if this is the *one*. *The* girl, or *the* promotion or *the* big win.

So this is one of the things I have to do to…to calm myself down.

DARWIN. Tell someone whether you'd fuck them?

RICHIE. Yeah.

No, not…

Not telling them. Telling…myself, or the universe or… I don't know. But saying it. So I know.

DARWIN. Can't you say it in your head?

RICHIE. Nah, it has to be out loud or it doesn't count.

DARWIN. According to who?

RICHIE. According to...

> (**RICHIE** *stares off into space for a second.
> Then he shakes it off and taps four times on
> the desk.* **DARWIN** *doesn't notice.*)

Like

,

What if the waitress is actually my soulmate, who I'm
supposed to be with? And if I didn't tell myself I'd want
her then, I might never... I might never be able to be
with her.

I might miss out.

> (**DARWIN** *sighs.*)

DARWIN. Did you do this with anyone else?

RICHIE. Stephanie. A bunch of 'no's for the men.

DARWIN. Do you do this with me? Like, every day?! I don't
want you thinking about –

RICHIE. No man, it's normally only with strangers. People
I know well are...already logged in the system.

DARWIN. So what, did you ever do this with my Mum?

> (*Beat.*)

RICHIE. Why would you ask that/

DARWIN. I'm just trying to understand/

You say this hasn't happened before but this has
happened shit like this keeps happening/

RICHIE. Can you not get pissed off?/

DARWIN. Why would I be pissed off? It's your life not mine.

RICHIE. You always get like this whenever I do something even a tiny bit 'weird' or... I, I can't be arsed to deal with it right now –

DARWIN. Come on man. All of these games you played as a kid, all of this "we're gonna be billionaires".

RICHIE. We both wanted that, that was what we –

DARWIN. When we were twelve!

I don't understand how you can be so...you're dating, you're working hard, you're so smart and then sometimes you just

You still act like a little kid.

,

Look man I'm sure you're gonna be happy and successful or whatever in the end but you're not gonna be a billionaire and you're not gonna miss out on your soulmate because you didn't tell them you'd fuck them.

Yeah?

(**RICHIE** *looks at the floor.*)

Yeah?

RICHIE. Yeah, alright. Yeah.

(*Blackout.*)

4.

(**RICHIE** *enters the basement, a little sullen.*
DARWIN's *on his feet. The filing cabinets and
chairs have been moved, switched up into a
bewildering Tetris combination that spans
the space behind them.*)

DARWIN. Morning!

(**RICHIE** *nods reluctantly.*)

I got something for you, are you ready?

RICHIE. Ready for what?

DARWIN. Ready for the fucking MORNING dude

RICHIE. You know I'm actually not feeling –

DARWIN. Shhh. Look. It's the perfectly optimised morning
routine.

Trust me you're gonna feel ready for anything. It's the
billionaire routine.

(**RICHIE** *cracks a slight grin.*)

RICHIE. Alright, try me.

(**DARWIN** *presses a button. Big music comes
on – something by Melt Yourself Down or
The Comet Is Coming.* *He starts moving to
the music,* **RICHIE** *follows. This time it's more
powerful. Pulsating. Swaying. Chest-forward.*)

DARWIN. Let's go. We wake up at four a.m., in the dark,
to get a headstart on the normies. Chug a full glass of
water. Gotta hydrate.

---

* A licence to produce *The Billionaire Inside Your Head* does not include
a performance licence for any third-party or copyrighted music or
copyrighted recordings.

(He hands **RICHIE** *a full pint of water.* **RICHIE** *looks apprehensive.)*

Come on time is money!! You've lost fifty million on the markets already!

*(***RICHIE*** *starts drinking.)*

Yesssss, all the way down.

*(***RICHIE*** *struggles but downs the water. Some of it spills over his face.)*

RICHIE. AAAgh!

DARWIN. Hydrated?

RICHIE. HYDRATED!

DARWIN. Alright now time to wake up the mind.

(He throws a copy of a newspaper at **RICHIE**.*)*

Just read the headlines, ten seconds GO.

*(***RICHIE*** *skim reading, yelling.* **DARWIN** *loudly counts down from ten.)*

RICHIE. STERLINGTUMBLESMARKETSINTURMOIL

(He flips the page.)

BITCOINUP30%NOWISTHETIMETOBUY

SCHRODERSASSETSPLUNGE£30BNASVOLA
TILITYCONTINUES, SELLSELLSELL

DARWIN. Time's up, you got it in your head? You know what's up?

RICHIE. I know what's up.

DARWIN. You know what's up?!

RICHIE. I KNOW what's up.

>   (**RICHIE** *throws the paper aside.*)

DARWIN. Then wake up your body. Military style obstacle course go!

RICHIE. What?!

DARWIN. Here! Up the table, onto the chair, jump to the cabinet, climb over, drop down, five burpees, run on the spot, vault the desk.

RICHIE. When did you even have time to –

DARWIN. YOU HAVE THIRTY SECONDS GO

>   (**RICHIE** *yelps and begins the course.* **DARWIN**
>   *turns up the music.* **RICHIE** *does well, but trips*
>   *over the final desk and falls flat. Meanwhile,*
>   **DARWIN** *picks up a huge bucket of ice water*
>   *from behind a cabinet.* **RICHIE** *does not see.*)

RICHIE. Fucking hell

DARWIN. Muscles pumping?

RICHIE. Muscles broken

DARWIN. Then rejuvenate your body with a ICE SHOWER

>   (**DARWIN** *pours the bucket over* **RICHIE.**
>   **RICHIE** *screams.*)

RICHIE. You fucking arsehole!!

DARWIN. Don't hate the player hate the game.

>   (**RICHIE** *picks up the bucket and sloshes the*
>   *dregs over* **DARWIN,** *laughing. They pant.*)

Feeling good, feeling awake?

RICHIE. Feeling like I'm gonna kill you

DARWIN. That's good, use that. Feeling like you got that billionaire grindset?

RICHIE. I fucking do.

> (**DARWIN** *stops the music.*)

DARWIN. Then let's get on with some work.

> (*Beat. Then they both burst out laughing.*)

RICHIE. You dickhead what was that??

DARWIN. Done my research ain't I.

> (**RICHIE** *looks at* **DARWIN**.)

RICHIE. Not bad.

For a normie.

> (**DARWIN** *grins, sits down and gets out rolling papers and small bag of weed.*)

Wait after that you're still slacking off?

DARWIN. Ey this was for you not me, my morning routine is still *Seinfeld* and a wank, thank you very much.

RICHIE. Can you imagine if Nicole came in now.

DARWIN. She never comes down here.

RICHIE. I know but imagine. What a state. Soaking wet. Flagrantly using drugs on company property.

DARWIN. Remember that time she caught us smoking on my roof?

RICHIE. Fuck man that was terrifying. Her just...standing over us.

DARWIN. Not saying a word. Never saying a word.

RICHIE. Just that look.

DARWIN. She was so good at that look. The furiously *disappointed* look.

RICHIE. Literally still gives me chills.

(Beat.)

DARWIN. How'd it go with her anyway?

RICHIE. What d'you mean?

DARWIN. The appraisal thing. I got mine tomorrow.

RICHIE. What, are you nervous? You're not exactly gonna fail it are you.

,

It was fine. Nothing much really. Just, pleased with your progress, keep it up, that kinda thing.

DARWIN. Could be worse. That was it?

*(Beat. **RICHIE** nods.)*

RICHIE. Maybe something like don't let my son flood the basement with an ice bucket?

*(**DARWIN** chuckles. Longer pause.)*

DARWIN. So she told me they're gonna hire a new Associate. Junior one.

*(**RICHIE** shifts a little, faux nonchalant.)*

RICHIE. Oh?

DARWIN. She said she mentioned it to you.

(Beat.)

RICHIE. Oh yeah. Yeah, she did.

Sorry/

DARWIN. Why didn't you say/

RICHIE. I dunno, it didn't...come up.

DARWIN. I'm telling you though, why wouldn't you –

RICHIE. Yeah I know, I don't know why... sorry.

DARWIN. Did you not want me to know?

RICHIE. No, I didn't not want you to know/

DARWIN. But you didn't want me *to* know either/

RICHIE. No, I...

,

I dunno, I didn't wanna make it weird.

DARWIN. Wouldn't have been weird if you'd told me.

> (**DARWIN** *looks at him curiously.* **RICHIE**
> *shifts a bit. But then* **DARWIN** *lets it go.)*

Nah I'm glad she told you. Otherwise it's like she'd told only me because I'm her son or something.

RICHIE. I mean of course she did. Business is ruthless, gotta give your blood a little heads up.

DARWIN. I guess. But she wouldn't... like she's obviously not gonna give me the job because of that.

RICHIE. Of course not man.

DARWIN. Obviously, that'd be fucked.

,

I don't even know if I want to apply anyway.

RICHIE. What you talking about, of course you do.

DARWIN. Why?

RICHIE. What do you mean why? It's, it's Associate. You get to put Junior Associate up, that's a sweet LinkedIn update if ever there was one.

DARWIN. I don't think there ever was one.

RICHIE. And big step equals big money.

DARWIN. What would I use it for, I don't need...

RICHIE. Now you're being ridiculous. You're sitting there in that peasant-from-the-1800s footwear and you tell me you don't need money?! That's how I know Nicole ain't giving you any allowance.

DARWIN. They're comfortable!

RICHIE. For a hobbit who's never worn shoes before sure!! Man you could get all new threads. Might even help you keep a woman around. I'll take you Moss Bros. Kit you out like an Executive.

>   (**DARWIN** *slaps* **RICHIE** *over the head with a folder and laughs.*)

DARWIN. So you found this Tommy Fox yet?

RICHIE. Yeaaaah boy, looks like the cunt is squatting in some warehouse.

DARWIN. If he's squatting in a warehouse he probably doesn't have this ten grand he owes does he?

RICHIE. Nah but they're meant to be nice about it, that was your mum's whole pitch right. Repayments not repossession. Genius.

DARWIN. *(Snorts.)* Changing the face of debt collection.

>   *(Beat.)*

You know I'm gonna tell her to give it to you.

RICHIE. What?

DARWIN. The promotion. I don't want it.

RICHIE. You serious?

DARWIN. *(Gesturing to his joint as he lights it.)* It's not like I deserve it.

RICHIE. You don't have to do that man, you have to at least apply –

DARWIN. Nah, it's nothing. I'll have a word.

RICHIE. *(Shaking his head.)* It's not fair on the others.

DARWIN. So what, it's their bad luck. Just your *good* luck to have the nicest best mate in the entire world, me. They'll get their turn, you'll just get there first.

RICHIE. Thanks man. But no. I gotta earn it.

You know that.

    (Beat. DARWIN *nods.)*

DARWIN. Maybe neither of us will get it. Maybe it'll go to...Gareth or someone.

RICHIE. Yeah right. Fucking thinks-Asia-is-a-country Gareth's gonna end up CEO of the world and we'll both be out on the street.

,

I'm only kidding.

DARWIN. What?

RICHIE. I'm only – I'm only kidding.

DARWIN. Yeah. I know. What? Why are you saying that?

Are you worried I'm gonna try and get Gareth promoted –

RICHIE. No, obviously not. I just...had to say.

DARWIN. Why?

RICHIE. I have to clarify sometimes.

That I was kidding.

DARWIN. For who? Who are you talking to?

The 'universe' again?

Seriously, who else is here that I can't see? Helloooo?

RICHIE. No one, it's just... don't, alright?

Sorry.

(*DARWIN steps closer to* **RICHIE***.*)

DARWIN.   Alright look. You can't... go with me here, I promise this will help. Okay? Say it again.

RICHIE. What do you mean?

DARWIN. The whole Gareth thing, say it again.

> (*Beat.* **DARWIN** *gestures for* **RICHIE** *to hurry up.*)

RICHIE. (*Hesitantly.*) Gareth will end up...CEO of the world. And we'll be out on the street.

DARWIN. Great, now don't say anything else.

> (**RICHIE** *is silent, but uncomfortable. His hands twitching.* **DARWIN** *waits, a hand by his ear as if waiting for a sound.*)

> (*After a few seconds* **DARWIN** *relaxes.*)

Ta-dah. Did anything happen? Did the sky fall in?

RICHIE. ...no.

DARWIN. We're still here, Gareth's still a useless cunt?

> (**RICHIE** *nods.*)

Right. Well done.

> (*He heads off.* **RICHIE** *stands alone. Confused. Like he can't remember how he got here.*)

> (*Blackout.*)

Interlude

(**THE VOICE** *bounds out onto the stage, addressing us.*)

THE VOICE. I've been thinking a lot about manifesting. Now I can see quite a few of you that are obviously into this – don't deny it. And yes, you are deeply embarrassing but look, I get it. It's a big trend. It's in vogue.

From what I could see there are two types of manifesting, right? Tell me if I'm wrong... actually don't contribute. Just listen.

There's the hippy dippy power of the universe, align the chakras in my arsehole kinda manifesting where you give yourself some mantras, repeat them over and over again, probably with some incense candle that smells like cum but cost you £65, and the universe will *grant* you your desires. Just like that.

Then there's optimising manifestation. I find this much more fun. You've seen those ads on Instagram, for whatever lifestyle app they're selling to the boys, they've all got pictures of that guy from *Peaky Blinders* after he's just beat someone to death and the caption is all "perfect yourself and the masses will fall in line" or something.

Well, yeah, if you've *murdered* someone, they probably will.

They say optimise yourself. Optimise your brain. Mindset, grindset, hustle, self-belief. Abstain from drugs and alcohol apart from Adderall Xanax and Valium. Wank in the shower while listening to an audiobook in each ear on double speed to save time.

They want you to clean your mind. Like it's the fucking filter on a hoover.

So write down your goals and chant them every day to yourself in the mirror. Convince yourself that this is what you are OWED, really, it's the bare fucking minimum of what you deserve. And there's no weird magic, no universal energy. Just efficiency. Focus. Profit.

Game the system. Dominate the competition. And you'll get everything you've ever been told to want.

'

Now I quite like that. I might want to have a play with it.

Just close your eyes for a minute and picture it. *It.* The future you need. The one where the world isn't on fire and your loved ones are alive and you haven't got that itching feeling like a spot under your tongue that none of this, none of this makes sense and maybe you don't want to be like the guy from *Peaky Blinders* even though the haircut is quite sexy and nothing you could ever achieve is going to stop your mind doing that thing where it squirms itself into a tangle so tight it can't breathe –

> *(She closes her eyes.)*

Picture a future where all that's melted away. Your perfect future.

Tell me about the house you're in. It's beautiful, isn't it? Modern? Art Deco? Cosy little Victorian cottage?

Mm. Nice choice.

What are you doing? Are you relaxing? Going for a swim? Writing the next great novel? Doing a few light Zoom calls on your investments and watching as the markets just...

> *(She moves her hand like a plane taking off with a whooooooosh.)*

Soar.

,

(She opens her eyes.)

Thing is, not to give the universe and all her chakras too much credit, but I think your thoughts and words *do* have power. In fact, I think all your wishes could come true...

If and only if you time them right.

Imagine it – if gods and particles and thought waves and dreams collided at one perfect moment, could you speak your happiness into existence? Could you change your future right then and there, just by saying it out loud? Maybe. Only problem with that is how are you gonna know when that 'perfect moment' is?

Was it when you told your love everything you ever wanted? When you described your perfect life, did the universe come together and say *yes*?

Or was it the time you told your mate, drunk-crying, you were gonna be alone forever? Was it when you told yourself in the mirror you've just realised you're going to die, and there's no way out?

Could you make that come true instead? With the power of your words.

Was it when you yelled at your parents, told them you wished they were dead?

(Faux dramatic.) Is that...why their car crashed?

,

You puny little shits will never know if or when your words have power. If or when I'll decide to *give* them power.

Is it today? Tomorrow? Never?

,

So if you're making a joke, and you say something you don't want to happen.

"Maybe I'll die tomorrow. Maybe I'll be out on the street."

How am I supposed to know you're not being serious? Why take the risk? Cos imagine how stupid (and how dead) you'd feel if it came true.

So just tell me, "I was only kidding". Out loud. Go on, tell me you're going to die tomorrow. Say it.

Say it.

> *(Beat. She listens. Maybe she picks on one of us in particular and asks again – say it.)*

Let it hang there for a second. A bit scary, isn't it? Leaving those words in the air. Poison fog.

Do you feel like it's closer to you than it was? Death?

Now don't worry. Just tell me – you were only kidding.

> *(She listens.)*

There we go. Not so hard. Now we're safe. Air cleared. All bases covered.

'

Remember that future. That wonderful future. Picture it. You only get one shot. Now you know what to do if you don't want to lose it.

Don't fuck it up.

> *(Blackout.)*

5.

(**NICOLE**'s *office. She's already seated as* **RICHIE** *enters.*)

NICOLE. Richard! Have a seat.

RICHIE. Richard, am I in trouble? Don't tell me, you found all the hobnob wrappers behind my desk and figured out who's been nicking the biscuits?

,

I don't actually... I only eat like three a day.

Four.

(**NICOLE** *smiles. Stillborn.* **RICHIE** *sits.*)

NICOLE. Good week?

RICHIE. Oh yeah, good week! Excited, you know, applying to be an 'associate' and all that.

NICOLE. Great.

So I just wanted to give you an update on the restructuring that we talked about previously.

RICHIE. Alright, nice one.

NICOLE. As you know, we looked at many options to see what's best for the company and all its employees, but in the end we've decided, me and the board, to shift focus away from tracking and research.

RICHIE. *(Not a clue.)* Right, got it.

NICOLE. I won't bore you with the details but the long and short of it is that we're going to be closing the Research team. Effective immediately.

(**RICHIE** *laughs.*)

Something funny?

RICHIE. Well you're joking, right, you're...oh. Sorry, so what are we gonna do? Are we moving out of the basement?!

NICOLE. No. Well, yes. Closing the team does mean the elimination of all Researcher positions, and unfortunately the restructuring has not allowed us to find any more available vacancies in other departments for internal moves.

RICHIE. Sorry I don't understand, what are we –

NICOLE. We're going to have to let the team go.

(*Beat.*)

RICHIE. You're firing me. Us. You're...

What about the Associate job?

NICOLE. I'm afraid that position's been filled.

RICHIE. But...

I don't understand. Did I do something wrong?

NICOLE. I'm sorry it's so sudden but I have no doubt you'll land on your feet. I meant everything I said in your appraisal, you're a great employee. And I'm sure you've been working towards launching your own thing. Maybe this is the time to take that to the next level.

(*Does she mean any of this?*)

RICHIE. I don't understand.

(**NICOLE** *leans forward. Puts a hand on* **RICHIE***'s shoulder. He stares at her hand in shock.*)

NICOLE. I wouldn't be here if my dad hadn't kicked me out. Put the fear of God in me, but it forced me to stand on my own two feet. Obviously I'm not saying this is the same, but.

Maybe this will be good for you, Rich. See what you'll do on your own.

RICHIE. What, what...

What about Tommy Fox?

NICOLE. Who?

RICHIE. Tommy Fox. He's a... he owes you ten grand, I found him in a warehouse in Harringay but I...

If if if I'm not here w-who's gonna contact him gonna get your money –

> (*As* **RICHIE** *babbles* **NICOLE** *shifts. The bouncy energy of an 80s Zumba teacher fills her body. She swings her feet up on her desk, kicking off her shoes. Maybe there's a lighting change. Maybe not. But* **NICOLE** *isn't here anymore.*)

THE VOICE. Eh, maybe she's right. Maybe this *will* make you realise the steps you need to take. To be successful. To be great.

RICHIE. *(Confused.)* Nicole?

THE VOICE. Or maybe this isn't what you need at all, maybe this is terrible but it's what you've got now isn't it because you didn't *listen* to me, did you, you never properly *listen*, you silly silly boy.

RICHIE. Nicole, what –

THE VOICE. Nicole isn't here right now, *Richard*, keep up!

> (**RICHIE** *looks up, startled.* **THE VOICE** *swings over the desk now, resting her shoeless feet on* **RICHIE**'*s thighs, sitting on the desk.*)

Richard. You know I knew something was up when she called you that.

THE VOICE. Now talk to me. Talk to me. You know what happened, right? You know why this happened.

RICHIE. The restructuring... it...

　　　　(**THE VOICE** *shakes her head.*)

THE VOICE. No, no, no. Come on sweetie. That's not it, is it.

　　　　(**RICHIE** *opens his mouth but* **THE VOICE** *presses a finger to his lips.*)

Just listen now. Just listen. It's okay. It's going to be okay. Silly Richie. Why can't you follow instructions? They're just simple instructions.

RICHIE. I didn't –

THE VOICE. Shh, it's alright. It'll be alright.

But I just need you to acknowledge, okay? That this happened, because you fucked up.

I didn't want this to happen. But I haven't got a choice, have I? You tell me you're going to be out on the street, what do you expect?

RICHIE. That wasn't, that wasn't... that was a joke, I –

THE VOICE. Well it's all very well and good telling me that now but you've already been fired, haven't you? No going back.

RICHIE. That's not why.

　　　　(**THE VOICE** *sits back.*)

THE VOICE. Sorry?

RICHIE. That's not why I got fired. She's...restructuring.

THE VOICE. (*Mockingly.*) "She's restructuring". So you think it's a coincidence?

RICHIE. What? No, it's not... she's restructuring, that's why. That is why.

THE VOICE. Just a coincidence that you tell me you're going to be out on the street, you don't *clarify*, you don't do what I told you, and you're let go? She just fires her best employee.

RICHIE. I'm not her best employee –

THE VOICE. With no warning. You think that makes sense?

RICHIE. No, but –

THE VOICE. No what?

RICHIE. No it doesn't make sense.

THE VOICE. Course it doesn't make sense.

RICHIE. It doesn't, it doesn't make sense I don't...fuck. FUCK.

> (**RICHIE** *stands up and starts pacing. Breathing heavily.*)

What am I going to do I can't... shit. Shit shit shit. I can't... I can't launch anything. I'm not ready. I can't even keep a job I can't do it I can't I –

> (**THE VOICE** *leaps down and grabs* **RICHIE** *by his shoulders.*)

THE VOICE. Stop it. Sit down.

> (*She pushes him to sit on the desk, and caresses his cheek.* **RICHIE** *is hyperventilating, on the verge of a panic attack.*)

It's going to be okay, Richie. Take deep breaths okay, just take a deep breath.

> (**RICHIE** *tries to take a breath.*)

Good. Now another one.

> (**RICHIE** *takes another deep breath.*)

THE VOICE. Darling I'm going to need you to take four deep breaths okay? You remember, you remember what happens if you do something three times, don't you? You can't do that. Only four.

>   (**RICHIE** *takes two more deep breaths.*)

Good, very good. Four. Nice. That's better.

>   (**RICHIE** *nods.* **THE VOICE** *puts her hands behind his neck.*)

Now put your left hand on the desk.

>   (**RICHIE** *puts his left hand on the desk.*)

Now your right hand.

>   (**RICHIE** *puts his right hand on the desk.*)

Slide your hands so they just meet the edge of the desk.

>   (**RICHIE** *does so.*)

Too far. Bit further back.

>   (**RICHIE** *slides them back.*)

Now tap for me. You can do that, can't you? It's going be okay, I just need you to tap for me.

Four times. Both hands. Simultaneously.

>   (**RICHIE** *taps four times.*)

That's better, isn't it?

>   (**RICHIE** *nods, eyes closed.* **THE VOICE** *caresses his cheek. Speaks into his ear.*)

Tap again. Four times.

>   (**RICHIE** *does so.*)

It's going to be okay. You're going to be okay. This changes nothing. You think I'm going to abandon you because of a little fuckup like this? Do you?

RICHIE. I... no. No you're not.

THE VOICE. That's right. I'm right here. I'm not going anywhere.

I've put a lot of work into you, you know.

> *(She chuckles.* **RICHIE** *smiles. She grabs his head, suddenly intense. Their faces close together.)*

There's a very rich man inside you, Richie. Inside that crazy head of yours. A good man. An ambitious man. A man who knows exactly what it is he's going to do when he wakes up every morning, and a man who does exactly that.

And what does he have to worry about?

RICHIE. Nothing.

THE VOICE. That's right.

> *(***THE VOICE** *walks behind the desk. She stands behind him. They both face us. She knocks on his head.)*

Now he's trying to get out. He's trying to get out but he's locked in. And all you've got to do to set him free. To *be* him...

> *(Tenderly, she strokes his face back to his hair. She pulls his hair back, slowly but forcefully until his entire head is pulled back.* **RICHIE** *gasps. He can't move.)*

is follow my *fucking* instructions. My clear and simple instructions.

(**THE VOICE**'s *other hand moves to* **RICHIE**'s *jaw. Holding it up. Holding it closed. Gripping.*)

THE VOICE. Have you got that? Or do I need to tell you again?

(**RICHIE** *tries to speak but he can't. He nods.* **THE VOICE** *relaxes her grip into a hug. An arm round his chest, a hand on his shoulder. She points at us.*)

Look at the mirror there. Look.

Show me what you'll look like when you let him out. When it's all settled down. When you've made it.

Smile like you've made it.

(**RICHIE** *smiles weakly.*)

No. Show me the face of a winner, Richie.

,

Look. Look at the mirror. That's you. You look like you're about to shit yourself. I thought you wanted to be a billionaire.

RICHIE. I do. I will be.

THE VOICE. Will you? Because that's your future you're looking at right now. Is that really what you want it to be?

RICHIE. No.

THE VOICE. What do you want to look like?

RICHIE. A winner.

THE VOICE. Then tell me you're a winner.

RICHIE. I'm a winner.

THE VOICE. No. Again.

RICHIE. I'm a winner.

THE VOICE. I don't believe you. Show me the face of a champion.

> (**RICHIE** *tries to smile more confidently.*)

RICHIE. I'm a winner.

THE VOICE. Again. A what?

RICHIE. A fucking winner.

THE VOICE. Again. Show me your billions. Come on.

> (**RICHIE** *grins confidently. He winks.*)

RICHIE. I'm a fucking winner.

THE VOICE. Four times. Tell me.

> (**RICHIE** *stands up.* **THE VOICE** *lets him go. He shouts.*)

RICHIE. I'm a fucking winner.

> ,

I'm a fucking WINNER.

> (*He paces forward.* **THE VOICE** *smiles and leaves, collecting her shoes.*)

I'M a fucking WINNER.

I'm a fucking WINNER.

> (**RICHIE** *stops, panting. He looks around – no one there.*)

> (*Blackout.*)

6.

(NICOLE and DARWIN's house. A dinner table. The two of them lay the table together for three, in complete silence. Sometimes, DARWIN looks at his mother. Opens his mouth to speak – then stops. NICOLE never reacts. It's unclear if she's ignoring him, or just hasn't noticed.)

(As they finish, NICOLE walks back the other way, and corrects DARWIN's place-setting. A knife askew. A glass rotated. Then DARWIN finally blurts it out.)

DARWIN. I still don't understand why you've invited him.

NICOLE. Because it would be nice to see how he's getting on.

(Off DARWIN's look.)

You're still friends, aren't you?

DARWIN. Yeah, we...

,

I haven't properly spoken to him. He's gone a bit AWOL.

NICOLE. Well, now will be a good time to catch up then.

DARWIN. Right. It's been weird, that's all.

NICOLE. *(Genuinely confused.)* Why?

(No answer. There is a knock on the door. NICOLE gestures to DARWIN and leaves. DARWIN goes to let RICHIE in. He's got a bottle of wine, a bouquet of flowers, and a nervous, excited energy.)

DARWIN. Hey.

RICHIE. Big D!

DARWIN. What?

(Gesturing to the flowers.) Please tell me those are for me and not my mum.

>   *(**RICHIE** pulls **DARWIN** into a hug.)*

RICHIE. Come here man, it's nice to see you.

>   *(He presses the wine into **DARWIN**'s hand and pushes past him to the table.)*

My my, got the nice silverware out. You still haven't changed these curtains then?

>   *(**DARWIN** follows.)*

DARWIN. Richie, I've been trying to text you, I…

>   *(**RICHIE** turns.)*

I'm so sorry. It's so fucked up, and I had no idea what she was going to do, you have to believe me. She never –

RICHIE. Ey of course you had no idea it's alright. It's alright.

DARWIN. It's not really though is it. Gareth was crying. Actually weeping. That bit was actually pretty funny. But –

RICHIE. Mate, please. Things happen for a reason right, what happens happens what's done is done we just gotta move. And trust me we are moving!

DARWIN. Right. But are you…are you okay?

RICHIE. *(Laughing.)* I've had better days at work man! But I'm good, honestly. It'll be alright, it'll be alright.

>   *(He taps four times.)*

DARWIN. Aren't you… I mean aren't you angry?

(RICHIE shakes his head, grinning.)

DARWIN. I tried to speak to her. I did, I tried but –

RICHIE. Don't do that bro. Please don't worry about me, this is just...just my next phase coming up a bit sooner than anticipated. The company gotta do what the company gotta do.

And don't worry for yourself as well yeah? I'm sure she's gonna find somewhere for you, she ain't gonna let her son down like that. If she hasn't already she'll find a little job for you someplace. Yeah?

*(He claps **DARWIN** on the shoulder reassuringly.)*

DARWIN. I –

RICHIE. This is nice of her though. You know, coming for dinner. Water, bridge, all that.

Sorry I went a bit off grid, had to for a few days you know just clear my head. Now I've been making moves I've been making plans I've been...commandeering my mind palace.

And this is where I'm meant to be.

DARWIN. Richie I need to tell you –

*(**NICOLE** comes back in, carrying wine glasses.)*

NICOLE. Rich! So lovely to see you.

(They embrace.)

RICHIE. Thanks so much, thanks for having me Nicole. It is such a pleasure to be here.

NICOLE. Of course. Oh wow, are those for me?

(She takes the flowers and admires them.)

They're beautiful. They even match my outfit.

RICHIE. Now that ain't no accident!

Well no I didn't mean, it is an accident obviously, I didn't... I didn't know what you'd be wearing, but it's lovely, really suits you –

DARWIN. *(To interrupt.)* I'm opening the wine.

> (**NICOLE** *puts the flowers on the side.* **DARWIN** *opens the wine and pours. They sit.*)

NICOLE. The food'll just be another few minutes.

RICHIE. Can't rush greatness!

> *(They lapse into a long silence.)*

NICOLE. So, how have you been?

RICHIE. I am glad you asked Nicole, you know I have been good. Very good. Because, and I'm just gonna jump right to the chase here I hope you don't mind?

> (**NICOLE** *shakes her head.*)

Well it's been a bit of a week for me obviously. But I was thinking about what you said in my, what shall I call it my, my *exit interview* and I was thinking you're right.

NICOLE. *(She always is.)* I am?

RICHIE. I've gotta make this the best thing that's ever happened to me.

When Zuckerberg dropped out of Harvard he was failing all his classes, there's no right time to... I'm saying I'm gonna fucking *launch*, my own company, right now, and go to the fucking moon. Now I've got pitches I've got ideas I've got products and/

DARWIN. Oh god/

RICHIE. I was wondering if I could run some by you, you know just for advice or maybe even a cheeky email address or two.

DARWIN. Mate is dinner the best time to do this –

RICHIE. Course it is D, course it is. Always mix business and pleasure.

> (*Beat.* **DARWIN** *drains his wine and looks for an excuse.*)

DARWIN. I'm gonna check on the food.

> (*He leaves.* **NICOLE** *just stares at* **RICHIE** *expectantly. Before it can get awkward –*)

RICHIE. So there's actually a startup incubator in, in L.A. that I was thinking of applying for. It's seed funding, you know and a six month programme, and I thought maybe you would be able to write me a reference.

> (*Beat.* **NICOLE** *doesn't respond. Just takes a sip from her wine. Suddenly it's all a bit real for* **RICHIE**. *He gulps. Leans forward, taps four times on the table.*)

Sorry now I'm saying that out loud maybe this isn't the best moment to ask...cos I don't want you to think I'm *demanding* anything, or...

> (*He taps four times again. Not enough, so he touches the backs of all the chairs he can reach.*)

Or...

Shit, I – I practiced this, I wrote it down so I wouldn't...

> (**RICHIE** *tails off. He doesn't know where to look.* **NICOLE** *is silent. Then, maybe the light shifts.*)

THE VOICE. Do you ever wonder why you picture me as her?

RICHIE. What?

> (*Beat.* **RICHIE** *looks at* **NICOLE**. *Something's off. It's not* **NICOLE** *anymore.*)

THE VOICE. Nicole. You've always pictured me as her, haven't you? Except with a little more *vavavoom*.

RICHIE. *(Whispers.)* Can you...can you not right now, I'm trying to –

THE VOICE. Did you have a crush on her? How very Mrs Robinson.

RICHIE. *(Whispers.)* No, I didn't have a crush on her.

THE VOICE. Oh but you do, don't you. You know you've told me you'd fuck her.

RICHIE. *(Whispers.)* Why would you do this right now? I'm trying to... I'm trying to pitch, it's going really well –

THE VOICE. Is it?

> *(***THE VOICE** *gestures to the chair* **NICOLE** *– they – are sitting in.)*

Then why isn't she saying anything? Sounds like you might've fucked up. Picked the wrong moment. Or freaked her out touching all her chairs like a weirdo.

God, why did you do this at dinner, *so* uncomfortable...

RICHIE. Can you fucking leave it, I'm trying to do what you want –

THE VOICE. Why are you letting me distract you then? How do you think you're gonna make it if you can't function under pressure? Keep going!

> *(Beat.* **RICHIE** *takes a breath. He knuckles down. He speaks confidently, staring straight ahead.)*

RICHIE. I'm asking for a reference because I really think I can get a place. I've got a background in crypto or friends in crypto anyway and that's one of the briefs they're looking for/

THE VOICE. Bit weird isn't it, to fancy your best friend's mum/

RICHIE. *(Through gritted teeth.)* They've got ten slots and three are reserved for new technology, which my pitch would fit into.

THE VOICE. *(Sings.)* Darwin's Mum has got it going on...

Do you think it's normal, how much you think about having sex with women?

RICHIE. I –

> *(He whispers again, an angry hiss.)*

I don't know, how much does everyone else think about it?

> *(**THE VOICE** shrugs.)*

THE VOICE. I don't know. But I know you think about it a lot.

Sorry why the fuck did you stop? Because I asked you a question? Or are you thinking about sex so much you can't even string a sentence together?

> *(**RICHIE** takes a deep breath and starts pitching again. He's speaking too loudly.)*

RICHIE. Anyway, the reason I'm bringing this up now is that it's run by Stuart Hawthorne./

THE VOICE. Do you think about it with every woman you meet?/

RICHIE. I remember you saying you knew him back in the day/

THE VOICE. Pathetic. Just an insecure prick desperately imagining them with their clothes off/

> *(**RICHIE** stands up. He's speaking even louder, staring straight ahead.)*

RICHIE. A reference would mean a lot coming from you, not not just because you know Stuart of course/

>(**DARWIN** *comes back in, carrying a lasagne. He stops in horror at* **RICHIE** *and stares.*)

THE VOICE. Do you see women as people or just… something to scratch an itch/

RICHIE. but because you're you you're a titan of industry or or and I know it's a bit weird because you've just fired me/

THE VOICE. Do you have any friends at all you haven't thought about fucking/

RICHIE. but I like to think you meant what you said about believing in me and/

THE VOICE. What about *your* Mum? Ever thought about fucking her?

RICHIE. SHUT UP! Shut up! Shut up!

>(**RICHIE** *barges backwards, putting his hands over his ears.*)

DARWIN. Mate are you alright –

>(**RICHIE** *goes straight into* **DARWIN**, *who drops the lasagne on the floor. It shatters.*)

>(*Long beat.* **RICHIE** *pants, calming down.* **NICOLE** *stands up and inspects the lasagne.*)

RICHIE. I'm so sorry I'm so sorry oh my god, I don't know what happened I'll, I bet we can clean it up I…

>(**NICOLE** *puts a hand on his shoulder.*)

NICOLE. I will write you a reference, Richie. A really fucking good one.

>(*She sits down. They follow.*)

RICHIE. Nicole I'm so sorry, I...

NICOLE. It's alright, Rich. You've had a rough week.

Maybe I should've realised that.

The last thing I would want is for there to be any weirdness between you two, what with Darwin staying on as Associate and all.

> *(The air goes out of the room.* **DARWIN** *looks down.)*

RICHIE. Darwin's... Darwin's the –

NICOLE. Associate. Didn't he tell you?

> *(They both look at* **DARWIN**.*)*

DARWIN. Richie, no this isn't...

I tried to tell you but I didn't want it to... I didn't want to be rude like I was rubbing it in your face. Because I wasn't, I...

I was trying to be nice.

RICHIE. Right.

Yeah.

,

Trying to be nice.

No, I guess it makes sense. You're the son, right? I figured she'd find a budget to squirrel you away somewhere, I did, or call up a mate to get you a job somewhere else that's just normal/

DARWIN. I'm sorry I never, I never meant it to be like this/

RICHIE. I guess what I didn't expect is for you to be hired as a fucking Associate, a job with actual meaningful responsibilities that actually have to get done, when you're the biggest fucking layabout in the whole building –

DARWIN. Dude –

RICHIE. *(To* **NICOLE**.*)* No I mean, you do know, don't you? That your new 'Associate' is high out of his skull every day in your office? That he even keeps the weed there so he doesn't have to do the taxing work of bringing it in in the morning? No, that would be far too much effort wouldn't it?

Is that the kind of company you want to run then? Is it?

> *(A long beat.* **NICOLE** *sighs.* **DARWIN** *leaves, making no attempt to clean up the mess.* **RICHIE** *eyes* **NICOLE**. *It feels like everyone's on thin ice now.)*

> *(***RICHIE** *looks at the lasagne.)*

RICHIE. Fuck.

NICOLE. Mmhmm.

You're going to have to apologise for that one.

God. Boys and their little spats.

'

You know, it makes me think.

> *(She pours another glass of wine.)*

I'm just not sure men can do this anymore.

RICHIE. Do what?

NICOLE. Lead.

> *(She stares at* **RICHIE**. *As if trying to figure him out.)*

It's like there's something wrong with you. You can't inspire. Motivate. Manage. Not in the way that I can.

NICOLE. I think it's that you've got too many instincts. Like fucking apes. Too much...anger! Fuck! Kill! Dominate! All primal reflexes, all the time, but no *thought*. No engineering.

> (**RICHIE** *opens his mouth but she cuts him off.*)

Sure, your style worked for a bit. But now it's run out of steam. I mean, look around. You aren't doing very well, are you? Men. All the drinking, all the violence. Killing women, killing each other, killing yourselves.

Not exactly the actions of a healthy group of people.

You see I'm rational, because I actually *feel* my emotions instead of just bottling them all into the first punch my little monkey brain wants to throw. I'm...connected to myself. Head and heart.

Are you connected to yourself, Richie? To all of yourself?

RICHIE. You don't...you don't think I can make it.

NICOLE. I don't know if you *can*. I'm just not sure you should.

> (*Beat.*)

RICHIE. So what should I...do then?

> (*Beat.* **NICOLE** *shrugs.*)

NICOLE. That's really not my problem.

> (*Blackout.*)

7.

*(Outside. **RICHIE** is shivering. **DARWIN** comes out and sits next to him.)*

DARWIN. Did you not bring a jacket?

RICHIE. I'm fine.

DARWIN. You're literally shaking.

RICHIE. I'm fine, I'm not cold.

DARWIN. Okay.

,

Do you want my jacket cos –

RICHIE. I said I'm not cold.

(Beat.)

DARWIN. I wish you hadn't fucking said that.

(Beat.)

RICHIE. What, that I'm not cold, why would I/

DARWIN. Obviously not that you prick/

Telling my mum I smoke at work.

RICHIE. Right, yeah. Me too.

,

(Unable to help himself.) It's not like she's gonna do anything though is it, not like she cares.

DARWIN. You don't know that. I could've lost my job.

RICHIE. You don't even want that job.

DARWIN. I still need it.

RICHIE. Do you?

DARWIN. I'm sorry. I didn't want to screw you over, but... it's rough out there right now. I gotta stick around. Until I figure out what I want to do next.

RICHIE. Until you figure out what you want to do next. Yeah. That's nice, that you can... yeah.

It'll be alright.

> *(He taps four times.)*

This is where I'm meant to be. I need to do this on my own anyway.

> *(An awkward beat.)*

DARWIN. Maybe you don't need to do it at all.

RICHIE. What?

DARWIN. Maybe this is a wakeup call. To just take it... cautiously right now...

> *(**RICHIE** shivers again.)*

and would you please take my fucking jacket before you freeze to the wall –

> *(**DARWIN** tries to take off his own jacket but **RICHIE** slaps his hands away.)*

RICHIE. No, leave it for fuck's sake! Nah man. Now's the time for a leap of faith. It's just hard graft.

> *(Beat.)*

DARWIN. Richie you don't have a job. Shouldn't you find one instead of applying for some incubator thing that... do they even pay you enough to move to the U.S.?

RICHIE. I'll figure it out.

> *(He taps four times.)*

DARWIN. You can't treat life like this...game you can just play and win. It doesn't work like that –

RICHIE. I'm not playing I'm working, I'm working hard and I'm not giving up –

DARWIN. Maybe you should give up! Because my Mum has just fired you for no visible reason at all and you need to realise that the world is not fair and isn't going to reward you for playing by this bizarre set of rules that you seem to have made up in your head.

RICHIE. I haven't made anything up I just *know* I can work and I can achieve –

DARWIN. You could work your whole life and not achieve anything and then one day you could just...get hit by a car and die.

RICHIE. But you can't live like that. You don't think I can make it but that's honestly not my problem because I, I believe in myself and I'm gonna take a chance, I'm gonna take a risk –

DARWIN. But this is not the time to take a risk –

RICHIE. It's what your mum would do.

DARWIN. Oh for fuck's sake –

RICHIE. What? It is. She fucking gambled everything on herself, and she won! *That* is confidence. That's hard work.

Come on, don't you want to...I dunno, do what she did?

DARWIN. No, I fucking don't! I don't *want* to do anything!

(*He turns to go, then spins back.*)

Also, for what it's worth, she got lucky. That's it. Luck.

She was in the right place at the right time, with the right idea. That's not genius, that's luck, and I wish everyone would stop going on about it. There were a million women like her with exactly the same skills and the same *drive* or whatever you keep saying but where are they? Nowhere because they didn't walk into a bathroom at the same time as an investor, or a start a business that ticked a load of that government's boxes, or have baby *me* to use as a fucking child sympathy card.

*(Beat. **RICHIE** deflates.)*

RICHIE. Wow.

DARWIN. Richie I'm trying to be nice. I don't want you to die broke in a ditch. And I'm sorry but the truth is you have never had a viable business idea in your life.

RICHIE. You don't mean that.

DARWIN. I do. So please listen to me, I'm begging you. This will not work, and you will fail.

(Long beat.)

RICHIE. You're kidding.

DARWIN. I'm not.

RICHIE. Tell me you're kidding.

DARWIN. Oh for fuck's sake.

RICHIE. Tell me you didn't mean that. That I'll fail.

Tell me you're kidding. Please.

DARWIN. No. I'm not kidding. You need to grow up.

*(**RICHIE** taps four times.)*

RICHIE. I just need you to tell me you're kidding then it'll be okay, please –

DARWIN. Snap out of it. Stop tapping it's like you're in a cult –

*(**RICHIE** goes to tap again and **DARWIN** slaps his hand away.)*

RICHIE. Leave it man I just need to... it just helps.

DARWIN. It doesn't help. It doesn't help, you are a fucking child. Taking a stupid risk doesn't help. Believing in your ideas past all logic and reason doesn't fucking help!

RICHIE. No what doesn't help is you stopping me from... from clarifying about Gareth and us being out on the street when I was kidding I was *KIDDING* but you didn't let me say and now look what's happened –

DARWIN. Are you serious right now? Have you actually lost your mind?

You think you were fired because I stopped you from telling *yourself* you'd made a joke about...about Gareth?

(**RICHIE** *sags a bit. He knows how it sounds.*)

RICHIE. ...you don't get it.

DARWIN. Oh I don't get it. What don't I get?

(**DARWIN** *lurches forward and 'grabs'* **RICHIE***'s nose like before, thumb between the fingers and waves it around.*)

Do I not get that this is really your nose but isn't but is but it's still on your face but it's in my hand, am I on the right track now?

(**DARWIN** *'drops' the nose onto the ground and stamps on it.* **RICHIE** *looks at the floor.*)

Come on, doesn't this make you feel weird? Aren't you gonna pick it up? Isn't this your worst nightmare or something?

RICHIE. I just need you to back me right now man, I need you in my corner –

DARWIN. Oh so you want me to back your stupid financial decisions and delusional ambition but I can't interrogate you needing to tell someone you'd fuck them?

RICHIE. Because that's *my* thing –

DARWIN. It's your thing that *I* have to deal with, that I have to watch, because I'm your friend and I care because I'm trying to help.

Can you understand that? Please tell me you can.

> *(Long beat.* **RICHIE** *nods, defeated.)*

THE VOICE. *(Offstage.)* What the fuck do you think you're doing?! Are you gonna let him talk to you like that?

> **(THE VOICE** *strides on, addressing* **RICHIE**, *who just shrugs, despondent.* **DARWIN** *waits for* **RICHIE** *to reply.)*

Some stoned prick who's never believed in you raises his voice *one time* and you just fall to pieces? When did you get so fucking fragile?

DARWIN. Richie?

RICHIE. He's just trying to help.

THE VOICE. Is he helping. Is this helping?

> *(***RICHIE** *shakes his head.* **DARWIN** *snaps his fingers in front of* **RICHIE**'s *face. He gets nothing.)*

DARWIN. This is real Rich –

RICHIE. He doesn't want me to waste my life.

THE VOICE. What the fuck do you think I want?! You could do SO much and instead you're...wilting like a *delicate little flower*.

DARWIN. Will you say something?/

RICHIE. I just... I thought you said I was a winner –

THE VOICE. *You* said you were a winner. Clearly you didn't mean it. Are you even trying? Are you even angry?

DARWIN. Dude, what the fuck/

RICHIE. I'm upset.

THE VOICE. You're angry at Nicole?

> (**RICHIE** *nods.* **DARWIN** *can't believe* **RICHIE** *is still silent.*)

DARWIN. Are you even listening to me?!

THE VOICE. You're angry at Darwin.

RICHIE. He's right –

THE VOICE. I didn't ask whether he's right, I asked whether you're angry at him.

> (*Beat.* **RICHIE** *considers.* **DARWIN,** *still getting no response from* **RICHIE,** *steps back in shock.*)

RICHIE. I am, but –

DARWIN. Seriously?

THE VOICE. So fuck him.

RICHIE. Fuck him.

THE VOICE. Fuck her.

DARWIN. *(Turning to go.)* Fuck this.

RICHIE. Fuck the both of them.

Testing my fucking patience.

THE VOICE. Then why don't you tell him what you think?

> (**THE VOICE** *circles, a manic auteur director.* **RICHIE** *focuses on* **DARWIN** *and amps himself up.*)

(In **RICHIE***'s ear.)* Go for his mother.

RICHIE. Why...why should I listen to anything you say when you're such a two-faced liar? You complain about your Mum, you aaaaalways disagree with everything she does, you resent her for all the success she's had –

DARWIN. Leave my Mum out of this/

THE VOICE. Ooh that's a sore point! Look at him, he's gonna cry/

> (**DARWIN** *steps closer.* **RICHIE** *squares up to him.*)

RICHIE. And then you turn around and take the job anyway because at the end of the day you're always gonna go running back to Mummy aren't you

DARWIN. Fuck off, man/

THE VOICE. Don't let up now, he's on the fucking ropes/

RICHIE. Always got your little safety net so you don't actually have to try and achieve *anything* with your life so don't come for me just because I've got ambition!

> (**THE VOICE** *punches the air triumphantly.* **DARWIN** *turns away, a little broken.*)

DARWIN & THE VOICE. (*In unison.*) This is embarrassing.

THE VOICE. Are you even fucking pissed off because right now feels like you're about to cry you wimp.

RICHIE. I *am* pissed off.

> (**THE VOICE** *pushes* **RICHIE,** *hard.*)

DARWIN & THE VOICE. (*In unison.*) Are you?

> (*He shoves her back.*)

RICHIE. Yeah. I fucking am, actually. Don't try me.

DARWIN & THE VOICE. (*In unison.*) Don't try you?

THE VOICE. Oh now you don't wanna be tried? Suddenly you don't wanna be tried?

RICHIE. No, don't fucking try me

> (**THE VOICE** *slaps* **RICHIE.**)

THE VOICE. *He's* fucking trying you, what do you want to do to him?

RICHIE. I...I wanna punch him.

I mean how fucking dare he how dare he speak to me like that.

I could kill someone –

THE VOICE. You wanna kill someone?

RICHIE. Yeah I wanna kill someone.

THE VOICE. Say it four times. I could kill him.

RICHIE. I could kill him.

I could kill him.

I could *kill* him.

DARWIN & THE VOICE. *(In unison.)* Say it again.

THE VOICE. Say it one more time or you'll end up in prison you fucking pussy

RICHIE. I could kill him!

DARWIN & THE VOICE. *(In unison.)* You haven't got it in you, you useless perverted little freak show –

> *(**RICHIE** screams and charges at **DARWIN**, tackling him to the ground. He punches **DARWIN**. Again. Again. Until he stops moving.)*
>
> *(He stands up. Panting. **THE VOICE** comes up behind him. She turns him. Kisses him. Long, slow, and passionate.)*
>
> *(After a beat **THE VOICE** releases **RICHIE** and he sits on the floor. Breathing slower now. **DARWIN** remains on the floor nearby. **THE VOICE** follows and puts her hands on his shoulders. Tender. Massaging.)*

(When she thinks he's calm enough:)

THE VOICE. Do you remember when you went to New York?

*(**RICHIE** looks at her, curiously.)*

(Gesturing to us.) Why don't you tell them about it?

Go on, they'll love it. Don't be shy. It's a great story.

*(**RICHIE** takes a deep breath.)*

RICHIE. I was eight.

THE VOICE. Six hour flight.

RICHIE. It didn't feel like a place could be that far away and be real, like...like I don't think I believed the plane actually moved before I got on. I thought they just kept it in the hangar, rolled screens past the windows, and then pretended we were somewhere else

But my mum promised it was real, a whole new...

Darwin had never left the country then and I remember bragging like I'm gonna be on a whole new continent

THE VOICE. What happened on the flight?

*(**RICHIE** speaks slowly, like he's only just now remembering.)*

RICHIE. My mum was worried I'd get all annoying so she gave me, gave me a sleeping pill. Or half of one. Snuck it into my Pepsi so none of the flight attendants would judge her

I went out like a light I don't even remember taking off.

THE VOICE. Did you dream?

When you slept, did you dream?

(Beat.)

RICHIE. *(Uncertain.)* Yeah. Yeah I...

Usually when I was a kid I'd always dream about teeth, like teeth falling out or living in a city made of teeth... that was a mad one –

THE VOICE. Richie. What did you dream on the plane?

RICHIE. Sorry yeah. It was different. I'm in like...an opera house. Or...a palace. I don't know. But there's like bare gold everywhere and paintings on the walls. And I'm wearing a suit and those sunglasses Robert Downey Jr. wore in Iron Man, I think I'd just been to see it.

And then the opera house or whatever started to melt. Like, from the ceiling all the gold and that just pouring down into liquid on the floor a whole hot lake underneath our feet and everyone starts panicking like well this isn't supposed to happen are we all gonna die

I mean I've never been to an opera house but I assume it isn't supposed to fucking *melt*

Anyway so everyone's freaking out right but I just stand there, smiling as it covers my shoes thick like syrup, and I remember thinking that I was the only person who knew what was going to happen next. And, for some reason, that was *very* important.

So everyone's panicking but when they see me...they all stop. Because *they* know *I* know what's going to happen. So if I'm not freaking out, why should they? And they smile at me. They nod at me, shake my hand as the walls collapse...

And then the gold melts down all over us and we're swimming in it, splashing in it like a pool and everyone's laughing and screaming with like, so much *happiness*. All because of me.

THE VOICE. Did it feel good?

RICHIE. Yeah. It felt great.

THE VOICE. And then you woke up?

> *(Beat.)*

RICHIE. I wake up and it's... the pilot's speaking over the intercom but I can't hear it, it must've been what woke me up but the whole plane is...

Shaking. Turbulence. It's rattling, that horrible metal rattling sound, bumping around like we're in a fucking washing machine

You know when you're much older and you think back and realise your parents have made a colossal mistake?

Mine showed me *Lost* at the age of seven.

So I'm...

Even my mum is looking scared, she's gripping the armrest way too tightly and I'm pretty sure...

I'm pretty sure...

THE VOICE. You were going to die?

> *(Beat.)*

RICHIE. We were going to die.

THE VOICE. You were going to die.

> **(RICHIE** *nods.)*

So what did you do?

RICHIE. I...I don't know why, but I thought about Nicole. And then...

You.

THE VOICE. Me.

RICHIE. I thought of you.

THE VOICE. You thought of me.

RICHIE. And you told me –

THE VOICE. Hold the armrests. Look at the seat in front of you. Don't take your eyes off it. Don't look out of the window. Tap your fingers. Once, twice, three times, four times. You can do this, Richie.

Do it again, four times. Keep doing it. Don't look out of the window. Tell me you're going to see the Empire State Building tomorrow.

RICHIE. I'm going to see the Empire State Building tomorrow.

THE VOICE. Don't look out of the window.

RICHIE. Don't look out of the window.

(*Beat.*)

THE VOICE. And what happened?

RICHIE. The plane...didn't crash. It was just a bit of turbulence.

We landed, safely.

And I saw the Empire State Building.

THE VOICE. We did that. Together. Didn't we?

RICHIE. It's not like we flew the plane –

THE VOICE. Yes it is. We flew the plane. Safely.

(*Beat.* **RICHIE** *looks at* **DARWIN** *on the floor.*)

RICHIE. Is that a...

Is that a real memory? Did that...really happen to me?

THE VOICE. Does it matter?

RICHIE. Of course it matters. Did I really dream that, I... did I hurt Darwin?

THE VOICE. He's all that matters, Richie. The billionaire. The man you were always meant to become. The man swimming in gold who never worries about a thing. Don't you still want to make it? Don't you want to be him?

>(**RICHIE** *nods.*)

We're still flying the plane Richie, and *that's* where we're going. All this time we've been flying out of the storm, out of the panic and the rattle and the fall and into the dream. Together. And every day we get closer and every day the billionaire grows bigger inside your head.

But now he needs to be born. So you can live in that palace forever. So you can be who you were always meant to be.

You're so close baby. I just need you to do one last thing for me.

,

Let him out.

>(**RICHIE***'s head hurts. Like there's something inside it.*)

Let him out.

>(**THE VOICE** *chants like she's summoning. Maybe her voice gets louder. Maybe other voices join in – a Satanic chorus.*)

Let him out.

>(*Maybe she gestures to us – her loyal followers – to chant with her. Say it.*)

Let him out.

>(**RICHIE** *screams. He's not sure where he is.* **THE VOICE** *grabs his jaw and prises it open.*)

Come on, Richie. He's reaaaaaadddyyyyyy!

> *(She sticks her hand down his throat. He gags but she keeps it there, trying to pull something out. A sound comes out of* **RICHIE** *that he's never heard himself make. Low. Guttural. Angry.)*

Just relax, and push. Let him out, Richie.

Let him out Richie.

LET HIM OUT.

> *(The chanting builds to a climax...but* **RICHIE** *chokes and falls back onto the floor.* **THE VOICE** *gets up, shaking her hand, disgusted. Disappointed.* **RICHIE** *gets his breath back.)*

> *(He crawls to* **DARWIN** *on the floor and shakes him.* **DARWIN** *doesn't move.)*

RICHIE. Did I...did I hurt Darwin? That wasn't real, was it? This isn't real, I didn't really do that –

THE VOICE. Let's go again.

RICHIE. Did you make me hurt him? Tell me, did you make me hurt Darwin?

THE VOICE. D-d-d-does it matter?

RICHIE. Of course it matters it all matters I don't want to hurt him –

THE VOICE. *(Mocking.)* "Ooh I don't want to hurt him oh no!" Get over yourself. You think the billionaire cares about this?

> *(***RICHIE** *puts his head in his hands, shaking it. Then he looks to* **THE VOICE.***)*

RICHIE. *You* made me, you fucking made me, why would you do that?! I need you to stop I don't want you telling me what to do –

THE VOICE. Bullshit you don't. I'm trying to help you get what you want –

RICHIE. But I didn't want *that*! He's my best mate.

(*He looks to* **THE VOICE**.)

I don't want you in my fucking head anymore.

(**THE VOICE** *is quite taken aback to hear this. But she quickly recovers.*)

THE VOICE. Oh, you don't? Just like that? After everything it's *bye bye* because little mummy's boy got upset is it?

RICHIE. Get out, please, shut up and get the fuck out of my head I can't breathe

THE VOICE. I AM YOU, you fucking pillock! I can't "get out of your head"?! It's like you haven't even been paying attention...

You know what you are without me? Do you? You want to have a taste of what's underneath *me*?

Ohhhhhh Richieeeee. Do you feel like you're on a plane right now?

(*Everything changes. Where once was calm, is panic. Turbulence. Shaking. Crashing. Screaming.* **RICHIE** *is on a plane.* **THE VOICE** *is everywhere around him.*)

RICHIE. What's –

THE VOICE. The plane is crashing, Richie.

RICHIE. I can't breathe –

THE VOICE. What are you gonna do?

RICHIE. I can't breathe I can't breathe –

THE VOICE. Get the fuck up.

*(***THE VOICE*** grabs* ***RICHIE*** *by his hair or his ear and yanks him up.)*

RICHIE. This isn't real. This isn't real.

THE VOICE. No? Okay, just look away, just look out the window and pretend everything's fine and I'm sure your last few moments before we crash into the fucking ocean will be peachy. Go on, look –

(She whirls him towards us and pushes him forward.)

RICHIE. This isn't real, it's just a game. It's just a game we're playing.

THE VOICE. Of course it's a game you fucking idiot! It's all a game. You think wanting to be a billionaire isn't a fucking game?

Don't you get it yet? If you're not playing the game, Richie, if you're not winning...

Then all you have is this.

(She gestures around her, whistles and mimes the sound of a falling object.)

The panic and the rattle and the fear.

Just a little boy falling out of the sky.

*(***RICHIE*** *is frenzied. The noise is almost unbearable.)*

(She bends over ***RICHIE*** *on the floor.)*

So are you ready to get off the plane now darling? We can go back to normal, and then we'll try again.

*(***RICHIE*** *looks again to* ***DARWIN*** *on the ground. And slowly stands up.)*

RICHIE. No.

THE VOICE. What?

RICHIE. No.

THE VOICE. Don't be silly Richie. Just remember what I told you and we can get off the plane.

Tap four times. Do it. Right now.

> (**RICHIE** *doesn't move. It's clear there's an overwhelming urge to tap but he doesn't.*)

RICHIE. No.

THE VOICE. Tell me you're going to see the Empire State Building tomorrow.

> (**RICHIE** *says nothing, through gritted teeth.*)

Richie, tell me. You want to get off the plane, don't you? You have to get off the plane, you can't STAY here?!

RICHIE. Maybe I can. What if I did? Just like...stay here? Can I do that?

THE VOICE. No you can't, you stupid little boy, you're falling, you're crashing –

RICHIE. So?

Maybe I'll stay here. Maybe – maybe I'll fucking *live* here!

What are you really gonna do if I don't do what you say? Really?

> (**THE VOICE** *switches tactics and paws at him, desperate.* **RICHIE** *squeezes his eyes shut.*)

THE VOICE. Richie, we're a team, you and me. Aren't we? Aren't we doing this together? You, you think you're going to be anything without me?! You think you can do this without *listening* to me?

RICHIE. I...I don't know. But I can't do this anymore. Not your way.

THE VOICE. My way?! It was *our* way you selfish boy, you think you're going to be a billionaire without me?

I *was* the dream, Richie. A dream to help you MANAGE your stupid life. And I was THERE for you every single day when no one else was and now you repay me by spitting it all back in my face?!

You think you can just *not listen* to me? Not do what I say? You'll last five minutes before you come running back all *tap tap tap tap oh I'm so sorry please let me tap a thousand times and you'll forgive me.*

But I fucking won't forgive you. However much you beg.

> *(She slaps him in the face. The plane's noise steps up a notch.)*

You are *nothing* without me.

> *(She slaps him again. The engines screech.)*

Nothing special.

> *(She slaps him again. The plane is burning up.)*

Nothing at all.

> *(She pulls him up by the hair and cradles his face.)*

(Suddenly soft, caring, pleading.) So please don't do anything stupid Richie, please, just tell me you'll see the Empire State Building and we can get off the plane, come on baby do it, we can go back to normal I promise I'll be nicer this time maybe I was too hard on you I only wanted the best for you but I'll be sweet I'll be anything whatever gets you there whatever makes you –

RICHIE. NO.

> (**THE VOICE** *flips. The plane turns into a nosedive.*)

THE VOICE. Well what am I supposed to fucking do then? Where am I supposed to go, huh? I'm not fucking *leaving.*

Come on Richie, don't be an idiot. It's not too late. Not yet.

> (**RICHIE** *doesn't move. The plane is going to hit the ground. It's a game of chicken.*)

You know you're never going to amount to anything, don't you? You'll just be another loser. Another one of the ninety-nine-percenters that don't leave a single mark on this shitty little Earth.

You'll be forgotten before your corpse is even cold. You know that?

When you finally give it up and die, there won't even be a trace. Richie, there won't even be a fucking trace! Is that what you want?!

> (**RICHIE** *doesn't move.* ***The plane crashes.*** **RICHIE** *crumples to the floor.*)

> (*Then, everything is calm, just like that. The plane is gone.* **RICHIE** *stands. He looks down at himself, shaken but to his amazement, intact. His arms, working. His face, unhurt. Then he looks at* **THE VOICE.**)

> (*For the first time, she can't meet his gaze. She just looks at her shoes. There's a tremble in her tone like she's almost going to cry. Like she's been found out. Like she's afraid.*)

What a waste of my fucking time.

I had things I wanted to *do* today.

> *(She leaves, head down, not looking back.* **RICHIE** *just stares after her. He can't quite believe anything he's seeing.)*

> *(Blackout.)*

8.

*(**NICOLE**'s office. She sits, working. **DARWIN** sits, playing on his phone. It's the end of the day and he's got his jacket on. After a while –)*

NICOLE. When are you going to move out?

DARWIN. What?

NICOLE. With the new job, I'm paying you enough to move out now.

DARWIN. Do you want me to move out?

*(**NICOLE** doesn't respond. Maybe a tiny, almost imperceptible shrug.)*

I...hadn't thought about it.

*(**NICOLE** nods – okay. Goes back to her work. Silence.)*

NICOLE. Oh – Rich kept mentioning this file he was closing, Tommy Fox. He seemed upset about it.

(Beat.)

DARWIN. Okay.

NICOLE. He's dead.

DARWIN. Who?

NICOLE. The debtor. Tommy Fox.

There isn't much in the estate but we should be able to get a fair bit recouped if you speak to the executor quickly.

Send him a card when we've collected.

DARWIN. Send who –

NICOLE. Richie.

DARWIN. Oh.

Like a 'well done' card?

NICOLE. Like...a card.

> *(Beat.)*

DARWIN. Has he got any kids?

NICOLE. Who?

DARWIN. Tommy Fox.

NICOLE. I think so. Why?

DARWIN. It doesn't sound like he had much, I mean... is it fair that we... before his kids...

I mean what are we realistically going to collect from him now?

NICOLE. Whatever we can.

> *(**DARWIN** opens his mouth to respond, but finds he can't even be bothered. Beat.)*

DARWIN. Okay. I'm going to go carry on clearing out the basement.

> *(**NICOLE** does not respond.)*

Then I'll probably leave.

> *(**NICOLE** does not respond. **DARWIN** is frustrated.)*

Then I'll take a shit on your desk.

> *(**NICOLE** looks up, eyebrows raised. Beat.)*

Why did I get this job?

NICOLE. What do you mean?

DARWIN. Why did I get the job? The promotion. Why me?

NICOLE. You're my son.

    (Beat.)

DARWIN. So I wasn't the best candidate? The only one worth keeping out of the whole team? You don't... believe in me?

    (Beat.)

NICOLE. *(Like it explains everything.)* You're my son.

DARWIN. Right. I'm just...your son.

Of course.

    (Beat.)

Why don't you talk to me?

    (**NICOLE** *looks up, a little annoyed now.)*

NICOLE. Why don't you talk to me?

DARWIN. I'm a surly young adult, I'm meant to not want to talk to you.

NICOLE. Then why do I have to talk to you?

DARWIN. Because you're my...

You can't talk to me but you'd give me a job?

NICOLE. I'm trying to get you where you need to be. That doesn't need talking.

You're my son.

DARWIN. But...

NICOLE. This is what people do, Darwin.

DARWIN. According to who?

Seriously.

Who made up these rules? Who told you to follow them? Why do you listen to them?

NICOLE. What's got into you?

DARWIN. What's got into me?! I dunno maybe, firing my best mate and, and then inviting him to some weird fucking dinner I mean I –

I don't know if I even want this job.

NICOLE. That's not what you said when I offered it to you.

DARWIN. No, that that, that was different though, that was before, it wasn't...

> *(He trails off. Bleeding out. He's got nothing. Long beat.* **NICOLE** *nods.)*

NICOLE. Right.

> *(Beat. She turns her head back to her work.* **DARWIN** *turns to go.)*

Oh, Darwin.

> *(***DARWIN** *stops.* **NICOLE** *does not look up.)*

Don't forget the card.

> *(Blackout.)*

9.

*(**RICHIE** sits facing us. Spotlighted. In an interview. He's not like we've seen him before. Shaky. Jumpy. Looking around to see if someone's listening. She isn't.)*

RICHIE. About myself? Yeah, yeah of course.

And you want me to say this, for the, for the camera, yeah? Yeah. Okay.

Hi, I'm, I'm Richie, and I'm gonna be the next big thing.

I think I've always been creative you know, since I was a little kid always creative always thinking outside of the box, ideas and that.

Used to come up with little schemes with my best mate at school. Getting up early to buy sweets from the local shop, selling them at twice the price in the playground. You know chatting shit all "we're gonna be billionaires when we grow up" ha.

,

Just...just kids being stupid really.

But yeah I always wanted to come out here, to L.A., to the land of the free, and do things properly. The big time. I always believed in myself see, my ideas, my ability with, with people you know to help them look at the world like I do. I wanted this so much I *knew* I'd make it happen.

I think wanting something that much is...safe, really. Isn't it? Safer than not wanting anything, anyway.

Cos it's not like... I know that if I make it big, if I make like, *billions*, it won't solve all my problems. Not really. I do know that.

But then I also kind of believe it will? Do you know what I mean?

I think our brains can do that right, they can have two thoughts at once, believe two things at once.

Like

,

Like

I have this...this voice in my head sometimes, not an actual voice I'm not crazy but sometimes it is a bit like an actual voice and it tells me, she tells me to do things like... I dunno, when I was a kid I had to say goodnight to all my toys in order, or my parents wouldn't wake up in the morning. Or get every word right singing along in the car or the car would crash.

Sorry that's a bit dark isn't it...

I know it's not real though, I do. I'm not mental. I know it's in my head, I don't believe the bad things would really happen, but, but like at the same time, I do? I really, completely do? Does that make sense? I mean fuck, sorry, I know it doesn't but it's...it's...

Fuck I sound mental, I –

> *(He tenses up. Sudden, rigid, eyes closed, like he's expecting a punch to the head. He breathes slowly, and after a few seconds opens his eyes again.)*

Sorry.

I didn't mean... sorry, can I, can I start that one again?

Yeah.

Thanks.

,

I'm Richie, and I'm gonna be the next big thing. Always been creative, having ideas, yeah said that, already, erm...

Well ideas aren't everything, are they? They're just ideas! But I've...I've always been driven to see them through to fruition. Yeah. Driven. Ambitious. I think that's what makes me stand out really, that's...

,

Well. I thought it did. I sort of...don't know now. Recently...

I always thought I was ambitious or passionate or special or *something* but actually it turns out, it turns out underneath

I'm just really scared.

,

I think I'm just really scared, all the time.

I'm scared of dying I'm scared of failing I'm scared of not leaving a mark on, on history or on anyone's heart I'm scared of this interview, fuck, no, that bit didn't come out like I...

Sorry, can I, can I go one more time? I'm sorry, I've just been a bit off today reckon it's the sun yeah haha. Silly Brit not used to the heat, I'm such a cliché yeah haha

So can I just...?

Thanks. Thank you. Thank you.

,

I'm Richie, and I'm gonna be the next big thing.

    (Blackout.)

10.

(The basement office. Even more decrepit than usual. It doesn't look like anyone's been down here for months.)

*(**RICHIE** comes in and switches on the single light. He's in casual clothing and a backpack.)*

*(If we look closely, we might realise **THE VOICE** is curled up on top of the filing cabinets in the back of the room. She seems to be sleeping.)*

*(**RICHIE** takes in the room slowly. He goes to his desk and packs away a few mementos into the rucksack. He goes over to the filing cabinets. Slowly pats them four times – 'good job'.)*

(Then he stares at Darwin's desk. He walks over and opens the drawer, pulling out Darwin's weed. He looks at it like he's never seen it before.)

DARWIN. Hey.

*(**RICHIE** jumps out of his skin. **DARWIN** is at the edge of the room, in a smart suit. Maybe his hair is a bit different.)*

RICHIE. Fuck me man you scared the shit out of me!

DARWIN. Sorry.

,

Thanks for coming.

(A long beat.)

RICHIE. Yeah, well.

Nice to see the old place.

DARWIN. Thought it could be cool. Remember all the fun we had here.

You know.

> (*A long beat.* **DARWIN** *looks at the weed in* **RICHIE**'s *hands.* **RICHIE** *remembers it's still there.*)

RICHIE. Ah yeah, I...think I was sort of wondering if you still kept it there.

If this place had changed.

> (*They both look around.*)

DARWIN. Like fuck it has.

It's like they've completely forgotten it's down here. They keep saying they're gonna move the files upstairs but another week goes by and...nothing.

RICHIE. I, I guess you're upstairs now and all, fancy new office yeah?

DARWIN. It's alright.

RICHIE. "It's alright", ah he says "it's alright" bet you got a nice swivel chair now though yeah? *Ergonomic.*

> (**DARWIN** *smiles.* **RICHIE** *gestures to the suit.*)

And the threads. Moss Bros?

DARWIN. Something like that.

> (**RICHIE** *fidgets and puts down the weed.*)

RICHIE. Saw you got a new title as well. What was it, Director/

DARWIN. Junior Director/

RICHIE. Still Director.

LinkedIn must've gone fucking wild.

(**DARWIN** *laughs.*)

Please tell me you understand how debt is bought now at least?

DARWIN. Ha. I do.

Well, mostly.

,

It's been months, dude.

(**RICHIE** *shrugs.*)

I haven't...haven't heard anything. No message, no update... come on.

(**RICHIE** *is silent.*)

Tell me, the incubator thing, you had the interview in L.A. right?

RICHIE. Oh yeah yeah yeah, that was well nice man! I tell you the beaches alone made that worth the trip, they're unreal.

DARWIN. Yeah? Nice one, did it, did it go –

RICHIE. Oh, no no no. Erm, very bad. Sort of

> (*He tenses up. Sudden, rigid, eyes closed, like he's expecting a punch. Breathing deeply.* **DARWIN** *goes towards him but then stops, unsure.*)

> (*Slowly,* **RICHIE** *opens his eyes.*)

Sorry. Just need a second.

I've been getting a bit...panicky. Bit *aaagh* you know, so I, so I sort of blew it.

RICHIE. Sort of came across like I was having a meltdown
,

Which makes sense, really

DARWIN. I'm sorry.

RICHIE. Least I got a nice holiday out of it. Expensive one, but still

>   *(Beat.)*

DARWIN. So what's next?

RICHIE. What's next?

Well.

I cashed out all my remaining money, got a flight to LAX, one way. I'm gonna go straight to the SpaceX headquarters, that's where Elon is most days at the moment, and I'm gonna bluff my way into the lobby, maybe the lift, and I'm gonna pitch to him straight up, gonna give him the old Richie charm, I won't take no for an answer, he'll be buying up forty-nine percent of my brain before you can say 'financial regulator'. Done deal.

>   *(Beat. **DARWIN**'s jaw has dropped in horror.*
>   *He looks at **RICHIE** who remains deadpan,*
>   *until –)*

D I'm fucking with you.

DARWIN. Oh my god/

RICHIE. The look on your face!!/

DARWIN. I mean can you blame me?!/

RICHIE. No, I am not doing that. Maybe some day.

For now I've been doing some bar work. Security you know, I'm actually pretty dece at it –

(He steps forward, hand out, firm tone.)

"Sorry mate not tonight."

(He shrugs – 'how's that?' **DARWIN** *grins.)*

That's...that's it. For now.

(Beat. **DARWIN** *steps closer.)*

DARWIN. Look Rich I, I asked you here to offer you a job.

RICHIE. What?

DARWIN. To give you a job back, I guess. It's high up, safe, stable. The company's in a much better position now. Working under – working in my team.

RICHIE. Thanks D but, I'm alright. Really.

(Beat.)

DARWIN. But this would be safe, Richie. Easy. Good salary, quick promotions. Swivel chair, right? Moss Bros, fucking Savile Row if you want.

RICHIE. I said no mate.

DARWIN. Don't be stupid. I know you're gonna say you need to "earn it yourself" or whatever bullshit moralising you're on now but when has that ever mattered really? I mean, really.

You only had the job in the first place because you grew up with me and you know that, deep down really, nobody 'earns' it themselves, not really, do they? They just get given it.

And I'm giving it to you. So take it. Please. Let me do this for you.

,

Come on, you don't want to be a fucking bouncer, you wanna be a –

RICHIE. I don't fucking want it!

,

(Firmly.) It's not good for me, D. It's not good for me.

Don't you know that by now? Don't you? If it's fucking obvious to me, it should be obvious to you. It's not good for me.

> (**DARWIN** *steps closer, cautiously.* **THE VOICE** *wakes up and crawls along the cabinet, watching.* **RICHIE** *twitches a bit.*)

DARWIN. Mate are you okay? Is this your... is it because of your thing?

RICHIE. *(Shouting.)* Why do you keep saying that! It's not a fucking "thing" D, it's not a... it just makes me feel like I'm safe.

,

Like if I do what it says, exactly what it says, I'll be completely in control of what happens to me. Like I'm actually holding my future in my hands.

But it's so *fragile*. It's so easy to break that I'm like, paralysed.

,

You ever feel like that?

> *(Beat.)*

DARWIN. No.

> (**RICHIE** *sits down on the floor. Exhausted.*)

Look I'm...

I'm sorry for being a dick about it.

RICHIE. Yeah well I'm sorry for telling your mum you're cosplaying as Snoop Dogg down here.

(Beat. They both laugh. **DARWIN** *walks around to the filing cabinets. He touches one, pausing.)*

DARWIN. You know Tommy Fox is dead?

RICHIE. Swear down? Shit.

What a waste of time.

DARWIN. I guess.

,

I never liked holding these.

RICHIE. What?

DARWIN. The files. When we had to pick them out. It's...

Each one of these is a person right, they're like... someone's entire life, their past like all their decisions all their experiences, through their money...

Tommy Fox. Or whoever. These are actual people but, but their entire futures are decided by how quickly us two idiots could find a file, pull it out, track them down, get their money back.

(He pulls a file out of the cabinet and holds it like a baby.)

Like you said, it's fragile. Holding that just feels... wrong.

*(***RICHIE*** gets up and takes the file from him.)*

RICHIE. Yeah.

Like, like maybe this kid wants to be a, a scientist or something and this is the difference between that and a whole other path for them like –

(He puts the file half back in the drawer.)

Now this kid's going to uni...

(He pulls it half out again.)

RICHIE. Now they "just can't make it work". Bad luck!

*(**DARWIN** takes the file.)*

DARWIN. Yeah but then I got to thinking, and it's not luck is it.

RICHIE. What do you mean?

DARWIN. Well it was us. Picking the file out. Changing their future.

*(**DARWIN**'s voice starts to crack a little. For some reason this...hurts.)*

What happened to you wasn't bad luck. It was my mum.

What's gonna happen to these people isn't luck.

It's me.

*(**DARWIN** ponders, unsure. Then he suddenly RIPS the file to pieces.)*

RICHIE. Woah what the fuck are you doing?!

*(**DARWIN** tosses the shreds to the ground.)*

DARWIN. There you go. Chances are whoever the fuck this is will never be found. Never have to pay anything back. Future changed.

Try it. Honest.

*(Long beat. **RICHIE** steps up, takes another file out of the cabinet. Looking to **DARWIN** almost for approval, he tears it in half. Then laughs. In surprise, at how easy it was. He tears it to pieces, laughing louder. He tosses the pieces up in the air and they rain down around them.)*

(Long beat.)

Hey.

*(He punches **RICHIE**'s arm affectionately.)*

I got something for you.

RICHIE. Trying to bribe me into this job?

DARWIN. No agenda. Promise. Just a present.

(He goes to a drawer and takes out something small, concealed in his hand. He walks over and opens his hand to reveal...nothing.)

RICHIE. What am I looking at here.

DARWIN. Dude. Don't you recognise it?

*(**RICHIE** shakes his head blankly.)*

It's your nose.

RICHIE. *(Starting to laugh.)* What?

DARWIN. After I ripped it off that time. I felt bad, you not being able to smell or anything.

I found it but it was pretty banged up. Sorry about that. So I took it to a guy. A nose-guy.

RICHIE. *(Laughing.)* A nose guy?

DARWIN. Yeah best one in the area. Five stars on Google. He gave it a clean, fixed it up. Good as new now he said. Smell better than ever.

You'll have the nose of a bloodhound now he said.

*(**RICHIE** laughs.)*

Yeah, bit of a strange man to be honest, I won't be going back. But –

*(**DARWIN** holds the nose up to **RICHIE**.)*

DARWIN. There you go. Look at that. Shiny, right?

RICHIE. A nose fit for a king.

,

You're holding it pretty tight there man.

> *(They both look at the nose. Then they look at each other.)*

DARWIN. Yeah, well. It's fragile. Gotta be careful not to break it.

> *(**DARWIN** 'hands' the nose to **RICHIE**, who takes it. Their hands linger. Long beat.)*

> *(**DARWIN** leaves.)*

> *(**RICHIE** sits alone, cradling his nose in two hands. His leg shakes a bit. **THE VOICE** pays attention. She dangles her legs over the edge of the filing cabinets. Watching him.)*

> *(**RICHIE** looks around the room. Smiles. Almost embarrassed. Stops smiling.)*

> *(He looks down at the nose. Maybe gives it a stroke.)*

> *(He sits like this for a long time.)*

> *(A looooong time.)*

> *(So long we're getting a bit restless.)*

> *(But **RICHIE** needs a long time right now. So he takes it.)*

> *(Finally, eventually, inevitably, he looks back at **THE VOICE**. She looks at him and shrugs with a smile. He turns away, and lifts up his hands.)*

(Carefully, delicately, he affixes the imaginary nose to his face. It's a perfect fit. He wrinkles it, maybe takes a test sniff. Feels great.)

*(**THE VOICE** smiles. **RICHIE** smiles back.)*

(Blackout.)

The End